THE DEFINING I AM JOURNAL

A DAILY GUIDE TO PERSONAL GROWTH, HEALING & SELF-LOVE

Created By:
VALERIE L. RICHARDS

Get in Touch

DEFINING I AM

www.definingiam.com
valerie@definingiam.com
@definingiam

Created & Designed by: Valerie L. Richards

ISBN: 978-0-578-46261-5

Manufactured in USA

What is so Special About This Journal?

• • • • • • • • • •

The DEFINING I AM Journal is not your average, fill in the blank, journal. It is a 12-week, daily writing guide that focuses on developing a mindset that cultivates Personal Growth, Positive Thinking, and Self-love.

Your mindset is a horrible thing to underestimate. It is the driver of the emotions, beliefs, and perceptions that ultimately influence how you view yourself and your life. This journal is unique because it is designed to teach you how to take control of your mindset and make it work for you. It will show you the power of gratitude and positive thinking. It will help you develop self-love through affirmation and encouragement. And you will see growth by facing your challenges, celebrating your wins and daring to dream big. Above all this journal is the perfect step to mastering a new way of thinking so you can master becoming the best you.

"You were created On Purpose, With a Purpose, For a Purpose."

-Valerie Richards

My Story

In the summer of 2015, I found myself in that all too familiar place of being sick and tired — of being sick and tired. I hated my job. I felt like my life was going nowhere. I struggled with self-doubt and self-worth. I was unhappy in my relationship. I felt fat and undesirable. I was just plain lost and hopeless. I knew I needed to make a change in my life, but I just didn't know how or where to begin.

One day, I felt that breaking point was getting too close for comfort. I was failing miserably at trying to fix things on my own, so I decided to seek counseling. After several unsuccessful attempts, I was introduced to self-help books. Before that, I was not much of a reader and knew nothing about the world of self-help. But I was at such a low point in my life that I was ready to try anything. Self-help turned out to be exactly what I needed. It set me on the path of healing, growth, and self-love that ultimately freed me from that dreadful sunken place. I learned the importance of meditation and journaling and incorporated them both into my daily life. For the first time in a long while, I felt optimistic about my future.

Journaling helped me to shift my mindset in a more positive and self-loving direction, and over time it taught me how to think, feel and do better for ME. It empowered me to live more authentically and go after my dreams. Meditation helped me to connect with God and address the pains and fears that were limiting me. It gave me an attitude of gratitude, which ultimately led me to discover my gifts and walk in my purpose.

I created **The DEFINING I AM Journal** because I want to share with others a little bit of what has changed my life for the better. I hope it will be a tool that guides you on your own journey of growth, healing, and self-love so you too can *define yourself for yourself*.

Dedication

• • • • • • • • • •

I dedicate this book to my legacy, Aysia, Kaylah, and Trinitee Lenore Richards. They are the reason I didn't give up on life. They are the reason I began this journey of personal growth, healing, and self-love; so that I may be an example and an inspiration for them to do the same for themselves. They are the reason you are reading this right now, about to embark on your own journey of *defining yourself for yourself.*

Love you Wodies. You all are my shining stars.

"It's not that you have to find the answer, you are the answer."

-Gary John Bishop

This Book Belongs to:

____

If found please contact me at:

____

and promise to keep everything read beyond page 35 confidential. A reward of $________ will be given for your silence and it's safe return.

Thank you.

Table of Contents

BEFORE YOU BEGIN: 15-33

THE JOURNAL: 35-183

"The meaning of life is to find your gift. The purpose of life is to give it away."

-Pablo Picasso

When God gave me the desire to create
The DEFINING I AM Journal I didn't know why and had no idea how.
All I knew was He wanted me to *do it* so He could *use it*.

So, scared out of my mind, I made the commitment to step out of my comfort zone, embrace the challenge and face the unknown.

As a result, I was able to make that vision a reality by which God has divinely chosen to share with you.

Now, there are very few guarantees in this world, and unfortunately, this book isn't one of them. But what I can say is if you are willing to get out of your comfort zone and commit to the process, you just might find yourself a little closer to living your best life.

You are not here by accident.
You do matter.
You do have a purpose.
You are ready.

"It's not the *will to win* that matters, -everyone has that. It's the *will to prepare* to win that matters."

-Paul Bear Bryant

BEFORE YOU BEGIN

5 Benefits of Journaling

• • • • • • • • • •

Journaling is an environment in which you *Become*.
-Valerie Richards

Many of us begin and end our days focusing on work, social media, kids, husbands, wives, etc. We spend little to no time fueling our mind, body, and spirit to help champion the day before us. As a result, over time, we end up losing sight of who we really are and what we really want. We get so engrossed in everyone else's needs and lives that we neglect our own and end up feeling lost, complacent and unhappy. Journaling can change that by helping you start and end your day in the best way. Here are 5 benefits that say how...

1. EVOKES MINDFULNESS

Being mindful is the human ability to be fully present and aware of yourself while not letting your surroundings overwhelm or distract you. Journaling requires you to focus on you and only you. You become fully present with your thoughts, feelings, behaviors, and desires, and in turn, learn how to love yourself better.

2. SUPPORTS ACHIEVING GOALS

Journaling often includes the writing of your dreams and goals. When you write things down, it signals your brain that "it's important." Subsequently, you become more aware of opportunities and tools that can help you achieve those goals.

3. STRENGTHENS SELF DISCIPLINE

Setting aside a regimented time each day for your self-improvement is an act of self-discipline. It's like exercising a muscle, the more you do it, the stronger you become, and over time it becomes a new healthy life habit.

4. GENERATES POSITIVE THINKING

This journal focuses on gratitude and self-love. When you are challenged to change the lens through which you see yourself and your life you begin to see that positive thinking is a choice. Life is 10% what happens to you and 90% how you handle it. Positive thinking helps you to better handle that 90%.

5. BUILDS SELF CONFIDENCE

Journaling about a positive experience allows your brain to relive it. It reaffirms your abilities and reminds you that, *You Can*, when self-doubt tries to discourage you. Remembering your victories will boost your self-esteem and mood and become a catalog of personal achievements that you can always revisit.

Success Plan

The key to success is to start before you are ready.
-Marie Forleo

Okay, I know what you're thinking. "Am I really ready to commit to this?" Look, being ready isn't some warm and fuzzy feeling in your chest, or a moment in time you're waiting on to arrive. It's simply the result of you making the decision to take action in spite of how you feel or the circumstances that surround you. It's a simple action, but not always an easy one. So try asking yourself another question, "Am I going to decide to do this?"

If you just said "yes" — *Congratulations, you just got ready!*

Now that you have made the decision to do this thing let's get you ready for success. I know you got this, but I do recommend you start by creating a personal Success Plan – don't worry, I got your back. Along the way, there may be some obstacles that will try to derail you. Creating a plan of action to deflect those obstacles is an excellent way to help keep you on track. So grab a pen and a beverage and, "Let's get it started. Oh-Oh Oh-Oh" (MC Hammer voice).

PART 1: Your Personal Statement

Sometimes what you think about yourself can be your biggest obstacle. If your thoughts are limiting and discouraging, your actions will be too. Part of you will want to move forward, but those thoughts will convince you that you can't. Learning to dispel those limiting thoughts is what's needed to shut them up, and prevent them from blocking your progress. So first, let's identify your limiting thoughts so you can then replace them with liberating and encouraging ones.

Identify:

List the top 3 limiting thoughts you struggle with.

1. ____________________________________
2. ____________________________________
3. ____________________________________

-Example-

1. *I don't matter so what's the point.*
2. *I don't have what it takes to change my life.*
3. *I am not good enough. I don't deserve better.*

Controlling the various thoughts that go through your mind on any given day isn't always easy, but changing them can be. Did you know, it is literally impossible to have two or more separate thoughts simultaneously. Don't believe me? — Okay, let's try it. Think about what you had for dinner last night *and* the last movie you saw at the same time — I'll wait. (Cue Jeopardy music please). Let me guess, you had to choose one or the other to start and then bounce back and forth between the two — right? "What's the point?", You ask. The point is your brain always gives you the ability to choose. If you have options, you can always choose the one that serves you best.

Dispel:

Replace your 3 limiting thoughts with liberating ones.

1. ______________________________
2. ______________________________
3. ______________________________

-Example-

1. *I am important and have a lot to offer.*
2. *I am strong and am in charge of my life.*
3. *My past does not determine my future. I deserve the best.*

Now that you have identified your limiting thoughts and dispelled them by creating liberating ones let's pull them together to form a Personal Statement. I encourage you to refer to it whenever you need to *change your mind*(set).

My personal statement is...

____

____

____

-Example-

I am important and have a lot to offer. God has given me the ability to make my life whatever I want it to be. I have left my past in the past and am focused on creating a better future.

PART 2: Your Shit Happens Plan

I can pretty much guarantee you that shit will happen and get in the way of your daily journal writing. That's okay, it's normal. But if you can identify the shit that is most likely to occur and find a way to block it from the fan or recover from the mess you stand a better chance at success. (Did I just get my Dr. Seuss on?)

List 3 turds that could hinder daily writing.

1. ____________________
2. ____________________
3. ____________________

-Example-

1. *I didn't hear my alarm and overslept.*
2. *I went out of town and left my journal at home.*
3. *I had a late night and passed out when I got home.*

List 1 way to block the turd and 1 way to recover from it.

1. ____________________
   ____
2. ____________________
   ____
3. ____________________
   ____

-Example-

1. *Write before you leave if you think you could be out too late.*
   Make time to complete both sections the next morning.

2. *Set a second alarm.*

Write anyway. You're already late and really need it now.

3. *Make it a part of your travel checklist.*

Keep a photo of the daily page in your phone to write from.

PART 3: Your Accountability Plan

Finding a way to keep yourself accountable is key to staying on track and committed to the journaling process. You can be as disciplined as you want to be, but it's always a good idea to have a support person or system in place. Here are a few suggestions for you to explore and choose from. Pick at least one, and note it as your accountability plan.

1. **Accountability Partner.** Find a close friend, family member or significant other that you can rely on to check in on you periodically. Let them know your journaling plan so they can be intentional about their accountability efforts.
2. **Accountability Calendar.** Purchase a wall or desk calendar and place it in a location you view daily such as the kitchen, your office or bedroom. Mark each day you finish.
3. **Accountability App.** You can use an app like *www.coach.me* or *www.stickk.com* that will help you track your goals and stick to your game plan.

My accountability plan is...

____

____

____

Journaling Guide

• • • • • • • • • •

Where God guides, He provides.
-Isaiah 55:11

The DEFINING I AM Journal is divided into weekly sections. Each week begins with a motivational message and challenge to prepare your mind(set). Then, you will be asked to define your personal focus for the week. Think about how you want to grow or heal. What goals do you want to achieve? What mindset do you want to develop? Change or repeat your focus as much as you like.

For each day, there is a morning and evening writing section. It is suggested that you make time to do both. However, if you are only able to commit to one or the other that works too. There is no right or wrong, just what's right for you. Here is a sample from my journal that you can use as a guide.

-Example-

Prepare Your Mind(set)

• • • • • • • • • • •

Self-love Challenge

The person you see in the mirror needs love, and you are the best person to give it. Take a little time, this week, to enjoy YOU. Pick one thing you've always wanted to try and just do it.

My personal focus for this week is *to develop a mindset that focuses on attracting the things into my life that make me happy, fulfilled and whole. I want to let go of the negative thoughts that are holding me back and keeping me from doing the things that will help me reach my goals.*

My challenge will be *to spontaneously try a new restaurant I've never been to before.*

Date: ____ / ____ / 20____

Good Morning Sunshine!

Waking up with gratitude cultivates a positive attitude. Think thankful.

I am grateful for my successful life coaching business.

NOTE: You can express gratitude for the past, present and also desires for the future.

It makes me happy when I am able to enjoy my morning cup of coffee, quietly and peacefully.

The most important thing you can wear is your confidence. Affirm yourself.

I love you Valerie
Your Name

You are an amazingly beautiful woman inside and out. Your kind and compassionate heart is what makes you a fantastic life coach.

Change is inevitable but growth is by choice. Be intentional.

Today I challenge myself to complete at least one lesson from my life coaching course work.

I proclaim that I am committed to the process of being a life coach.

RECITE ALL OF THE ABOVE 3 TIMES OUT LOUD

How was your day?

Remember today you just made history. Celebrate you!

A great experience I had today was going bowling with my family. We had fun talking and laughing at our horrible bowling skills.

Your future is counting on you to make the most of today. Be optimistic.

A challenge I had today was keeping my mind focused on the positive. I struggled with thoughts of self-doubt.

A Win I had today was completing a lesson from my life coach course.

I Dream of being a best selling author.

SPEND 5 MINUTES MEDITATING ON YOUR DREAMS

At the end of each week, you will find a "Weekly Recap" that consists of four review questions summarizing your journaling experience. I recommend taking a few extra minutes to complete it as a part of day seven's evening-writing.

Weekly Recap

Don't forget to stop and smell the roses.
-Walter Hagen

What was the highlight of your week?

Completing the next phase of my journal project, which was to put together a focus group.

How did you manage your "Focus" for the week?

This week I tried to create affirmations that were in line with my focus. Saying them helped when I had moments of frustration or doubt.

What were your top 2 Wins this week?

1. *Completing section two of my life coaching course.*
2. *Completing seven consecutive days of journaling.*

How did you complete this weeks challenge exercise?

This week I went to Wades, a new restaurant I have been wanting to try. I went by myself and had a great time with me.

Affirmation Guide

• • • • • • • • • • •

I love and approve of myself.
-Tiffany Haddish

An affirmation, in simple terms, is a statement that gives one a heightened sense of value and accomplishment. It is the barrier between the *subconscious limiting beliefs*, and *conscious liberating beliefs* we addressed in the Success Plan. Affirmations also increase the vibrations for happiness, appreciation, and gratitude that attract the people, resources, and opportunities you need to achieve your goals. Believe it or not, you already use affirmations every day, but the problem is they aren't always positive.

"I am never going to lose weight."
"I am so broke."
"I am never going to find love."

I am sure you have made one of those statements to yourself at some point in time. But the good news is you can easily change that. The morning section of the journal addresses self-affirmation by prompting you to speak loving and affirming words to yourself. Sometimes this can be a difficult transition so here are a few tips that can lead you in the right direction.

1. STAY PRESENT

Shift your mindset from the future tense to the present tense. Take something you desire and write as if you already have it.

"I am 20lbs lighter" not "I want to be 20lbs lighter."

2. STAY POSITIVE

Focus on what you *do* want, not what you *don't* want. Write in the positive tense. Our subconscious mind often skips the word **not,** so eliminate it from your affirmations.

"I am a confident public speaker" instead of
"I am not afraid to speak publicly."

3. NO BOUNDARIES

Look at an affirmation as a verbal expression of your personal, perfect world. Think outside of your current reality. You don't have to have it, be it or even fully believe it. It just has to be a positive statement that speaks to something you want for yourself and your life. Remember, there is no limit to what you can have or who you can be.

4. REMAIN GRATEFUL

Having an attitude of gratitude attracts great things into your life. It allows you to see the greatness that is already there and keeps you operating on a high frequency of positivity, happiness and self-love.

Affirmation Examples

- You are free from the pains of your past. They no longer have control over you.
- You are a big dreamer who chooses to make your dreams a reality.
- You are rich and have the abundant wealth to live the life of your dreams.
- Your presence is intentional. God created you on purpose, with a purpose, and for a purpose.
- You love yourself, inside and out, no matter what society and people say or think about you.
- You have an amazing body. People look at you in awe of your beauty and grace.
- You are a positive thinker who only speaks positively about yourself and others.
- You deserve a happy, loving and fulfilling relationship. You have high expectations for what you want and deserve.
- You are caring and respectful of your total health and have let go of unhealthy addictions.
- You are forgiving of those who have hurt you, including yourself.
- You are free from worry about the judgment and opinions of others.
- You are beautiful, confident, strong and loved.

Meditation Guide

If you don't control your mind, someone else will.
-John Allston

A part of this daily journal suggests meditating for five minutes before you end your day. I have been meditating daily for many years now and have seen tremendous results. Meditation is an experience that takes you to the core of who you are. It allows you to shut out the noisy, chaotic world around you and connect with self and your creator. It settles your thoughts and emotions. It reduces stress and anxiety. It helps you to release the past and find peace in the present. Essentially, meditation is a private tea party with your mind, body, and spirit. With that being said, meditation, in theory, is simple but is not always easy, so here are a few tips to get you started.

1. GET COMFORTABLE

Finding a comfortable position and place is key. Sitting with your legs crossed works, but you can also relax in a chair or lie down as long as your legs don't go numb and you don't fall asleep. A quiet place is also essential. It's hard enough to tame your inner thoughts, so try not to add outside noise to the mix.

2. NO EXPECTATIONS

Meditation is a practice. The more you practice and trust in the process the easier it becomes to tame the noise in your head, engage in the moment and reap the benefits. Some days you will feel better about your experience than others but don't let that discourage you. Remember, a few minutes of meditation is always better than none.

3. KEEP THOUGHTS MOVING

The hardest part of meditation is taming those darn thoughts. They swirl around your head, 24/7, like the damn Energizer Bunny. But the goal isn't to try and get rid of them. It's to wave at them as they pass by, and resist the temptation to invite them in for dinner. Let them pass and get back to meditating.

4. UTTER SOMETHING GOOD

Sometimes saying a mantra, prayer or short phrase helps to keep your thoughts focused. My personal go-to is, "Thank You, Lord," but you can choose anything that puts you in the right head-space and helps you stay connected to the experience.

5. REFLECT

Take a few moments to reflect on your meditation experience and write your thoughts on the note page located at the end of each weekly section. Ask yourself; How did meditating make you feel. Did you receive any guidance or clarity? Did you recognize a shift in your mindset or mood? Remember positive reflection creates repetitive action.

What are you willing to do, to be who you are meant to be?

IT TAKES CHANGE TO MAKE CHANGE.

My Commitment

• • • • • • • • • • •

Commitment is the glue that bonds you to your goal.
-Jill Koenig

Fill in your commitment statement below and read it whenever you need a little motivation.

I, ______________________________, commit to completing at least 12-weeks of **The DEFINING I AM journal**, starting ____________________.

I am committing to this because I ______________________________

____

When I complete 12-weeks of journaling I will treat myself by:

____

If, by chance, I don't complete 12 weeks I promise to:

____

I commit to the following daily journaling plan:

[ ] Morning When: ______________________________

[ ] Evening When: ______________________________

Signature: ______________________________ Date: ________________

"Everything you desire is, right here, right now. You just have to shift your perception in order to see it..."

-Jen Sincero

THE JOURNAL

You're either going to love yourself or hate yourself. Choose love– It feels better.

GIVE YOURSELF THE LOVE YOU GIVE OTHERS.

WEEK ONE

Prepare Your Mind(set)

• • • • • • • • • • •

Self-love Challenge

The person you see in the mirror needs love, and you are the best person to give it. Take a little time, this week, to enjoy YOU. Pick one thing you've always wanted to try and just do it.

My personal focus for this week is ____________________

My challenge will be ____________________

Date: ____/ ____/ 20____

Good Morning Sunshine!

Waking up with gratitude cultivates a positive attitude. Think thankful.

I am grateful for ______________________________

____

It makes me happy when ______________________________

____

The most important thing you can wear is your confidence. Affirm yourself.

I love you ______________________________
Your Name

You ______________________________

____

Change is inevitable but growth is by choice. Be intentional.

Today I challenge myself to ______________________________

____

I proclaim that I ______________________________

RECITE ALL OF THE ABOVE 3 TIMES OUT LOUD

How was your day?

Remember today you just made history. Celebrate you!

A great experience I had today was ______________________________

____

Your future is counting on you to make the most of today. Be optimistic.

A challenge I had today was ______________________________

____

A Win I had today was ______________________________

____

I Dream of ______________________________

SPEND 5 MINUTES MEDITATING ON YOUR DREAMS

Date: ____ / ____ / 20____

Good Morning Sunshine!

Waking up with gratitude cultivates a positive attitude. Think thankful.

I am grateful for ______________________________

____

It makes me happy when ______________________________

____

The most important thing you can wear is your confidence. Affirm yourself.

I love you ______________________________

Your Name

You ______________________________

____

Change is inevitable but growth is by choice. Be intentional.

Today I challenge myself to ______________________________

____

I proclaim that I ______________________________

RECITE ALL OF THE ABOVE 3 TIMES OUT LOUD

How was your day?

Remember today you just made history. Celebrate you!

A great experience I had today was ______________________________

____

Your future is counting on you to make the most of today. Be optimistic.

A challenge I had today was ______________________________

____

A Win I had today was ______________________________

____

I Dream of ______________________________

SPEND 5 MINUTES MEDITATING ON YOUR DREAMS

Date: ____ / ____ / 20____

Good Morning Sunshine!

Waking up with gratitude cultivates a positive attitude. Think thankful.

I am grateful for ______________________________

____

It makes me happy when ______________________________

____

The most important thing you can wear is your confidence. Affirm yourself.

I love you ______________________________
Your Name

You ______________________________

____

Change is inevitable but growth is by choice. Be intentional.

Today I challenge myself to ______________________________

____

I proclaim that I ______________________________

RECITE ALL OF THE ABOVE 3 TIMES OUT LOUD

How was your day?

Remember today you just made history. Celebrate you!

A great experience I had today was ______________________________

____

Your future is counting on you to make the most of today. Be optimistic.

A challenge I had today was ______________________________

____

A Win I had today was ______________________________

____

I Dream of ______________________________

SPEND 5 MINUTES MEDITATING ON YOUR DREAMS

Date: ____/ ____/ 20____

Good Morning Sunshine!

Waking up with gratitude cultivates a positive attitude. Think thankful.

I am grateful for ______________________________

____

It makes me happy when ______________________________

____

The most important thing you can wear is your confidence. Affirm yourself.

I love you ______________________________
Your Name

You ______________________________

____

Change is inevitable but growth is by choice. Be intentional.

Today I challenge myself to ______________________________

____

I proclaim that I ______________________________

RECITE ALL OF THE ABOVE 3 TIMES OUT LOUD

How was your day?

Remember today you just made history. Celebrate you!

A great experience I had today was ______________________________

____

Your future is counting on you to make the most of today. Be optimistic.

A challenge I had today was ______________________________

____

A Win I had today was ______________________________

____

I Dream of ______________________________

SPEND 5 MINUTES MEDITATING ON YOUR DREAMS

Date: ____ / ____ / 20____

Good Morning Sunshine!

Waking up with gratitude cultivates a positive attitude. Think thankful.

I am grateful for ______________________________

____

It makes me happy when ______________________________

____

The most important thing you can wear is your confidence. Affirm yourself.

I love you ______________________________
Your Name

You ______________________________

____

Change is inevitable but growth is by choice. Be intentional.

Today I challenge myself to ______________________________

____

I proclaim that I ______________________________

RECITE ALL OF THE ABOVE 3 TIMES OUT LOUD

How was your day?

Remember today you just made history. Celebrate you!

A great experience I had today was ______________________________

____

Your future is counting on you to make the most of today. Be optimistic.

A challenge I had today was ______________________________

____

A Win I had today was ______________________________

____

I Dream of ______________________________

SPEND 5 MINUTES MEDITATING ON YOUR DREAMS

Date: ____ / ____ / 20____

Good Morning Sunshine!

Waking up with gratitude cultivates a positive attitude. Think thankful.

I am grateful for ______________________________

____

It makes me happy when ______________________________

____

The most important thing you can wear is your confidence. Affirm yourself.

I love you ______________________
Your Name

You ______________________________

____

Change is inevitable but growth is by choice. Be intentional.

Today I challenge myself to ______________________________

____

I proclaim that I ______________________________

RECITE ALL OF THE ABOVE 3 TIMES OUT LOUD

How was your day?

Remember today you just made history. Celebrate you!

A great experience I had today was ______________________________

____

Your future is counting on you to make the most of today. Be optimistic.

A challenge I had today was ______________________________

____

A Win I had today was ______________________________

____

I Dream of ______________________________

SPEND 5 MINUTES MEDITATING ON YOUR DREAMS

Date: ____/ ____/ 20____

Good Morning Sunshine!

Waking up with gratitude cultivates a positive attitude. Think thankful.

I am grateful for ______________________________

____

It makes me happy when ______________________________

____

The most important thing you can wear is your confidence. Affirm yourself.

I love you ______________________________
Your Name

You ______________________________

____

Change is inevitable but growth is by choice. Be intentional.

Today I challenge myself to ______________________________

____

I proclaim that I ______________________________

RECITE ALL OF THE ABOVE 3 TIMES OUT LOUD

How was your day?

Remember today you just made history. Celebrate you!

A great experience I had today was ______________________________

____

Your future is counting on you to make the most of today. Be optimistic.

A challenge I had today was ______________________________

____

A Win I had today was ______________________________

____

I Dream of ______________________________

SPEND 5 MINUTES MEDITATING ON YOUR DREAMS

Weekly Recap

Don't forget to stop and smell the roses.
-Walter Hagen

Take a moment to reflect on this week's wins and challenges. If you need any personal coaching or guidance I'm only an email away.
valerie@definingiam.com

What was the highlight of your week?

____

____

____

How did you manage your "Focus" for the week?

____

____

____

What were your top 2 Wins this week?

1. ______________________________
2. ______________________________

How did you complete this weeks challenge exercise?

____

____

____

Notes

"Remember to celebrate milestones as you prepare for the road ahead."

-Nelson Mandela

Milestone Celebration

• • • • • • • • • • •

Congratulations you have just completed 1 week, 7 days and 105 hours of using **The Defining I Am Journal**. At this point, I hope you can say you are enjoying the daily writing and getting into a bit of a groove. Remember growth is a self-discovery process that is ever evolving, so be patient with yourself and...

KEEP GOING!

You cannot grow a positive mindset, using negative soil.

CHECK YOUR SOIL.

WEEK TWO

Prepare Your Mind(set)

• • • • • • • • • • •

Mindset Challenge

The messages you feed your mind are just as important as the food you feed your body. Take inventory of the messages you are exposing yourself to every day (friends, social media, TV). Find one that is not positively serving you and eliminate it this week.

My personal focus for this week is ______________________

____

____

____

____

____

This week I will eliminate ______________________

____

____

____

____

____

Date: ____/ ____/ 20____

Good Morning Sunshine!

Waking up with gratitude cultivates a positive attitude. Think thankful.

I am grateful for ______________________________

____

It makes me happy when ______________________________

____

The most important thing you can wear is your confidence. Affirm yourself.

I love you ______________________________
Your Name

You ______________________________

____

Change is inevitable but growth is by choice. Be intentional.

Today I challenge myself to ______________________________

____

I proclaim that I ______________________________

RECITE ALL OF THE ABOVE 3 TIMES OUT LOUD

How was your day?

Remember today you just made history. Celebrate you!

A great experience I had today was ______________________________

____

Your future is counting on you to make the most of today. Be optimistic.

A challenge I had today was ______________________________

____

A Win I had today was ______________________________

____

I Dream of ______________________________

SPEND 5 MINUTES MEDITATING ON YOUR DREAMS

Date: ____/ ____/ 20____

Good Morning Sunshine!

Waking up with gratitude cultivates a positive attitude. Think thankful.

I am grateful for ____

____

It makes me happy when ____

____

The most important thing you can wear is your confidence. Affirm yourself.

I love you ______________________
Your Name

You ____

____

Change is inevitable but growth is by choice. Be intentional.

Today I challenge myself to ______________________________________

____

I proclaim that I ____

RECITE ALL OF THE ABOVE 3 TIMES OUT LOUD

How was your day?

Remember today you just made history. Celebrate you!

A great experience I had today was _________________________________

____

Your future is counting on you to make the most of today. Be optimistic.

A challenge I had today was ______________________________________

____

A Win I had today was ____

____

I Dream of ____

SPEND 5 MINUTES MEDITATING ON YOUR DREAMS

Date: ____/ ____/ 20____

Good Morning Sunshine!

Waking up with gratitude cultivates a positive attitude. Think thankful.

I am grateful for ______________________________

____

It makes me happy when ______________________________

____

The most important thing you can wear is your confidence. Affirm yourself.

I love you ______________________________
Your Name

You ______________________________

____

Change is inevitable but growth is by choice. Be intentional.

Today I challenge myself to ______________________________

____

I proclaim that I ______________________________

RECITE ALL OF THE ABOVE 3 TIMES OUT LOUD

How was your day?

Remember today you just made history. Celebrate you!

A great experience I had today was ______________________________

____

Your future is counting on you to make the most of today. Be optimistic.

A challenge I had today was ______________________________

____

A Win I had today was ______________________________

____

I Dream of ______________________________

SPEND 5 MINUTES MEDITATING ON YOUR DREAMS

Date: ____/ ____/ 20____

Good Morning Sunshine!

Waking up with gratitude cultivates a positive attitude. Think thankful.

I am grateful for ______________________________

____

It makes me happy when ______________________________

____

The most important thing you can wear is your confidence. Affirm yourself.

I love you ______________________________
Your Name

You ______________________________

____

Change is inevitable but growth is by choice. Be intentional.

Today I challenge myself to ______________________________

____

I proclaim that I ______________________________

RECITE ALL OF THE ABOVE 3 TIMES OUT LOUD

How was your day?

Remember today you just made history. Celebrate you!

A great experience I had today was ______________________________

____

Your future is counting on you to make the most of today. Be optimistic.

A challenge I had today was ______________________________

____

A Win I had today was ______________________________

____

I Dream of ______________________________

SPEND 5 MINUTES MEDITATING ON YOUR DREAMS

Date: ____/ ____/ 20____

Good Morning Sunshine!

Waking up with gratitude cultivates a positive attitude. Think thankful.

I am grateful for ____________________

____

It makes me happy when ____________________

____

The most important thing you can wear is your confidence. Affirm yourself.

I love you ____________________
Your Name

You ____________________

____

Change is inevitable but growth is by choice. Be intentional.

Today I challenge myself to ____________________

____

I proclaim that I ____________________

RECITE ALL OF THE ABOVE 3 TIMES OUT LOUD

How was your day?

Remember today you just made history. Celebrate you!

A great experience I had today was ____________________

____

Your future is counting on you to make the most of today. Be optimistic.

A challenge I had today was ____________________

____

A Win I had today was ____________________

____

I Dream of ____________________

SPEND 5 MINUTES MEDITATING ON YOUR DREAMS

Date: ____/ ____/ 20____

Good Morning Sunshine!

Waking up with gratitude cultivates a positive attitude. Think thankful.

I am grateful for ____

____

It makes me happy when ____

____

The most important thing you can wear is your confidence. Affirm yourself.

I love you ______________________
Your Name

You ____

____

Change is inevitable but growth is by choice. Be intentional.

Today I challenge myself to ____________________________________

____

I proclaim that I ____

RECITE ALL OF THE ABOVE 3 TIMES OUT LOUD

How was your day?

Remember today you just made history. Celebrate you!

A great experience I had today was _____________________________

____

Your future is counting on you to make the most of today. Be optimistic.

A challenge I had today was ___________________________________

____

A Win I had today was ____

____

I Dream of ____

SPEND 5 MINUTES MEDITATING ON YOUR DREAMS

Date: ____/ ____/ 20____

Good Morning Sunshine!

Waking up with gratitude cultivates a positive attitude. Think thankful.

I am grateful for ______________________________

____

It makes me happy when ______________________________

____

The most important thing you can wear is your confidence. Affirm yourself.

I love you ______________________________
Your Name

You ______________________________

____

Change is inevitable but growth is by choice. Be intentional.

Today I challenge myself to ______________________________

____

I proclaim that I ______________________________

RECITE ALL OF THE ABOVE 3 TIMES OUT LOUD

How was your day?

Remember today you just made history. Celebrate you!

A great experience I had today was ______________________________

____

Your future is counting on you to make the most of today. Be optimistic.

A challenge I had today was ______________________________

____

A Win I had today was ______________________________

____

I Dream of ______________________________

SPEND 5 MINUTES MEDITATING ON YOUR DREAMS

Weekly Recap

Don't forget to stop and smell the roses.
-Walter Hagen

Take a moment to reflect on this week's wins and challenges. If you need any personal coaching or guidance I'm only an email away.

valerie@definingiam.com

What was the highlight of your week?

____

____

____

How did you manage your "Focus" for the week?

____

____

____

What were your top 2 Wins this week?

1. ______________________________
2. ______________________________

How did you complete this weeks challenge exercise?

____

____

____

Notes

"For change to work, ACTion is necessary."

Action Changes Things

-WE by: Gillian Anderson & Jennifer Nadel

WEEK THREE

Prepare Your Mind(set)

• • • • • • • • • • •

ACT Challenge

Sometimes the smallest action can have the most significant impact. Look at voting. The simple act of checking a box on a ballot ultimately determines the leader of the free world. Challenge yourself to ACT this week. Take one action that can help you move closer to a personal goal.

My personal focus for this week is ______________________________

____

____

____

____

____

I action I will take is ______________________________

____

____

____

____

____

Date: ____/ ____/ 20____

Good Morning Sunshine!

Waking up with gratitude cultivates a positive attitude. Think thankful.

I am grateful for ______________________________

____

It makes me happy when ______________________________

____

The most important thing you can wear is your confidence. Affirm yourself.

I love you ______________________________
Your Name

You ______________________________

____

Change is inevitable but growth is by choice. Be intentional.

Today I challenge myself to ______________________________

____

I proclaim that I ______________________________

RECITE ALL OF THE ABOVE 3 TIMES OUT LOUD

How was your day?

Remember today you just made history. Celebrate you!

A great experience I had today was ______________________________

____

Your future is counting on you to make the most of today. Be optimistic.

A challenge I had today was ______________________________

____

A Win I had today was ______________________________

____

I Dream of ______________________________

SPEND 5 MINUTES MEDITATING ON YOUR DREAMS

Date: ____/ ____/ 20____

Good Morning Sunshine!

Waking up with gratitude cultivates a positive attitude. Think thankful.

I am grateful for ____

____

It makes me happy when ____

____

The most important thing you can wear is your confidence. Affirm yourself.

I love you ____________________
Your Name

You ____

____

Change is inevitable but growth is by choice. Be intentional.

Today I challenge myself to ____

____

I proclaim that I ____

RECITE ALL OF THE ABOVE 3 TIMES OUT LOUD

How was your day?

Remember today you just made history. Celebrate you!

A great experience I had today was ____

____

Your future is counting on you to make the most of today. Be optimistic.

A challenge I had today was ____

____

A Win I had today was ____

____

I Dream of ____

SPEND 5 MINUTES MEDITATING ON YOUR DREAMS

Date: ____/ ____/ 20____

Good Morning Sunshine!

Waking up with gratitude cultivates a positive attitude. Think thankful.

I am grateful for ____

____

It makes me happy when ____

____

The most important thing you can wear is your confidence. Affirm yourself.

I love you ______________________
Your Name

You ____

____

Change is inevitable but growth is by choice. Be intentional.

Today I challenge myself to ______________________________________

____

I proclaim that I ____

RECITE ALL OF THE ABOVE 3 TIMES OUT LOUD

How was your day?

Remember today you just made history. Celebrate you!

A great experience I had today was ________________________________

____

Your future is counting on you to make the most of today. Be optimistic.

A challenge I had today was ______________________________________

____

A Win I had today was ____

____

I Dream of ____

SPEND 5 MINUTES MEDITATING ON YOUR DREAMS

Date: ____/ ____/ 20____

Good Morning Sunshine!

Waking up with gratitude cultivates a positive attitude. Think thankful.

I am grateful for ____

____

It makes me happy when ____

____

The most important thing you can wear is your confidence. Affirm yourself.

I love you ______________________
Your Name

You ____

____

Change is inevitable but growth is by choice. Be intentional.

Today I challenge myself to ____

____

I proclaim that I ____

RECITE ALL OF THE ABOVE 3 TIMES OUT LOUD

How was your day?

Remember today you just made history. Celebrate you!

A great experience I had today was ____

____

Your future is counting on you to make the most of today. Be optimistic.

A challenge I had today was ____

____

A Win I had today was ____

____

I Dream of ____

SPEND 5 MINUTES MEDITATING ON YOUR DREAMS

Date: ____/ ____/ 20____

Good Morning Sunshine!

Waking up with gratitude cultivates a positive attitude. Think thankful.

I am grateful for ____________________

____

It makes me happy when ____________________

____

The most important thing you can wear is your confidence. Affirm yourself.

I love you ____________________
Your Name

You ____________________

____

Change is inevitable but growth is by choice. Be intentional.

Today I challenge myself to ____________________

____

I proclaim that I ____________________

RECITE ALL OF THE ABOVE 3 TIMES OUT LOUD

How was your day?

Remember today you just made history. Celebrate you!

A great experience I had today was ____________________

____

Your future is counting on you to make the most of today. Be optimistic.

A challenge I had today was ____________________

____

A Win I had today was ____________________

____

I Dream of ____________________

SPEND 5 MINUTES MEDITATING ON YOUR DREAMS

Date: ____ / ____ / 20____

Good Morning Sunshine!

Waking up with gratitude cultivates a positive attitude. Think thankful.

I am grateful for ______________________________

____

It makes me happy when ______________________________

____

The most important thing you can wear is your confidence. Affirm yourself.

I love you ______________________________
Your Name

You ______________________________

____

Change is inevitable but growth is by choice. Be intentional.

Today I challenge myself to ______________________________

____

I proclaim that I ______________________________

RECITE ALL OF THE ABOVE 3 TIMES OUT LOUD

How was your day?

Remember today you just made history. Celebrate you!

A great experience I had today was ______________________________

____

Your future is counting on you to make the most of today. Be optimistic.

A challenge I had today was ______________________________

____

A Win I had today was ______________________________

____

I Dream of ______________________________

SPEND 5 MINUTES MEDITATING ON YOUR DREAMS

Date: ____/ ____/ 20____

Good Morning Sunshine!

Waking up with gratitude cultivates a positive attitude. Think thankful.

I am grateful for ______________________________

____

It makes me happy when ______________________________

____

The most important thing you can wear is your confidence. Affirm yourself.

I love you ______________________________
Your Name

You ______________________________

____

Change is inevitable but growth is by choice. Be intentional.

Today I challenge myself to ______________________________

____

I proclaim that I ______________________________

RECITE ALL OF THE ABOVE 3 TIMES OUT LOUD

How was your day?

Remember today you just made history. Celebrate you!

A great experience I had today was ______________________________

____

Your future is counting on you to make the most of today. Be optimistic.

A challenge I had today was ______________________________

____

A Win I had today was ______________________________

____

I Dream of ______________________________

SPEND 5 MINUTES MEDITATING ON YOUR DREAMS

Weekly Recap

• • • • • • • • • •

Don't forget to stop and smell the roses.
-Walter Hagen

Take a moment to reflect on this week's wins and challenges. If you need any personal coaching or guidance I'm only an email away.

valerie@definingiam.com

What was the highlight of your week?

____

____

____

How did you manage your "Focus" for the week?

____

____

____

What were your top 2 Wins this week?

1. ____
2. ____

How did you complete this weeks challenge exercise?

____

____

____

Notes

Untie the NOTs, and free yourself from your subconscious.

CHANGE IS A CHOICE MADE DAILY.

WEEK FOUR

Prepare Your Mind(set)

• • • • • • • • • • •

Belief Challenge

We are our own worst enemy. Well, really our subconscious is. It's the place that houses the negative beliefs we developed as a child and have been holding on to ever since.

"I am Not." "I canNot." "I will Not."

In order to improve your mindset you first need to untie those *Nots* by eliminating them. What are three *Nots* you will untie?

My personal focus for this week is ____________________

The NOTs I will eliminate are ____________________

Date: ____/ ____/ 20____

Good Morning Sunshine!

Waking up with gratitude cultivates a positive attitude. Think thankful.

I am grateful for ______________________________

____

It makes me happy when ______________________________

____

The most important thing you can wear is your confidence. Affirm yourself.

I love you ______________________________
Your Name

You ______________________________

____

Change is inevitable but growth is by choice. Be intentional.

Today I challenge myself to ______________________________

____

I proclaim that I ______________________________

RECITE ALL OF THE ABOVE 3 TIMES OUT LOUD

How was your day?

Remember today you just made history. Celebrate you!

A great experience I had today was ______________________________

____

Your future is counting on you to make the most of today. Be optimistic.

A challenge I had today was ______________________________

____

A Win I had today was ______________________________

____

I Dream of ______________________________

SPEND 5 MINUTES MEDITATING ON YOUR DREAMS

Date: ____ / ____ / 20____

Good Morning Sunshine!

Waking up with gratitude cultivates a positive attitude. Think thankful.

I am grateful for ______________________________

____

It makes me happy when ______________________________

____

The most important thing you can wear is your confidence. Affirm yourself.

I love you ______________________________
Your Name

You ______________________________

____

Change is inevitable but growth is by choice. Be intentional.

Today I challenge myself to ______________________________

____

I proclaim that I ______________________________

RECITE ALL OF THE ABOVE 3 TIMES OUT LOUD

How was your day?

Remember today you just made history. Celebrate you!

A great experience I had today was ______________________________

____

Your future is counting on you to make the most of today. Be optimistic.

A challenge I had today was ______________________________

____

A Win I had today was ______________________________

____

I Dream of ______________________________

SPEND 5 MINUTES MEDITATING ON YOUR DREAMS

Date: ____/ ____/ 20____

Good Morning Sunshine!

Waking up with gratitude cultivates a positive attitude. Think thankful.

I am grateful for ____

____

It makes me happy when ____

____

The most important thing you can wear is your confidence. Affirm yourself.

I love you ______________________
Your Name

You ____

____

Change is inevitable but growth is by choice. Be intentional.

Today I challenge myself to ____________________________________

____

I proclaim that I ____

RECITE ALL OF THE ABOVE 3 TIMES OUT LOUD

How was your day?

Remember today you just made history. Celebrate you!

A great experience I had today was _____________________________

____

Your future is counting on you to make the most of today. Be optimistic.

A challenge I had today was ____________________________________

____

A Win I had today was ____

____

I Dream of ____

SPEND 5 MINUTES MEDITATING ON YOUR DREAMS

Date: ____/ ____/ 20____

Good Morning Sunshine!

Waking up with gratitude cultivates a positive attitude. Think thankful.

I am grateful for ______________________________

____

It makes me happy when ______________________________

____

The most important thing you can wear is your confidence. Affirm yourself.

I love you ______________________________
Your Name

You ______________________________

____

Change is inevitable but growth is by choice. Be intentional.

Today I challenge myself to ______________________________

____

I proclaim that I ______________________________

RECITE ALL OF THE ABOVE 3 TIMES OUT LOUD

How was your day?

Remember today you just made history. Celebrate you!

A great experience I had today was ______________________________

____

Your future is counting on you to make the most of today. Be optimistic.

A challenge I had today was ______________________________

____

A Win I had today was ______________________________

____

I Dream of ______________________________

SPEND 5 MINUTES MEDITATING ON YOUR DREAMS

Date: ____/ ____/ 20____

Good Morning Sunshine!

Waking up with gratitude cultivates a positive attitude. Think thankful.

I am grateful for ______________________________

____

It makes me happy when ______________________________

____

The most important thing you can wear is your confidence. Affirm yourself.

I love you ______________________________
Your Name

You ______________________________

____

Change is inevitable but growth is by choice. Be intentional.

Today I challenge myself to ______________________________

____

I proclaim that I ______________________________

RECITE ALL OF THE ABOVE 3 TIMES OUT LOUD

How was your day?

Remember today you just made history. Celebrate you!

A great experience I had today was ______________________________

____

Your future is counting on you to make the most of today. Be optimistic.

A challenge I had today was ______________________________

____

A Win I had today was ______________________________

____

I Dream of ______________________________

SPEND 5 MINUTES MEDITATING ON YOUR DREAMS

Date: ____/ ____/ 20____

Good Morning Sunshine!

Waking up with gratitude cultivates a positive attitude. Think thankful.

I am grateful for ____

____

It makes me happy when ____

____

The most important thing you can wear is your confidence. Affirm yourself.

I love you ______________________
Your Name

You ____

____

Change is inevitable but growth is by choice. Be intentional.

Today I challenge myself to ____

____

I proclaim that I ____

RECITE ALL OF THE ABOVE 3 TIMES OUT LOUD

How was your day?

Remember today you just made history. Celebrate you!

A great experience I had today was ____

____

Your future is counting on you to make the most of today. Be optimistic.

A challenge I had today was ____

____

A Win I had today was ____

____

I Dream of ____

SPEND 5 MINUTES MEDITATING ON YOUR DREAMS

Date: ____/ ____/ 20____

Good Morning Sunshine!

Waking up with gratitude cultivates a positive attitude. Think thankful.

I am grateful for ______________________________

____

It makes me happy when ______________________________

____

The most important thing you can wear is your confidence. Affirm yourself.

I love you ______________________________
Your Name

You ______________________________

____

Change is inevitable but growth is by choice. Be intentional.

Today I challenge myself to ______________________________

____

I proclaim that I ______________________________

RECITE ALL OF THE ABOVE 3 TIMES OUT LOUD

How was your day?

Remember today you just made history. Celebrate you!

A great experience I had today was ______________________________

____

Your future is counting on you to make the most of today. Be optimistic.

A challenge I had today was ______________________________

____

A Win I had today was ______________________________

____

I Dream of ______________________________

SPEND 5 MINUTES MEDITATING ON YOUR DREAMS

Weekly Recap

• • • • • • • • • •

Don't forget to stop and smell the roses.
-Walter Hagen

Take a moment to reflect on this week's wins and challenges. If you need any personal coaching or guidance I'm only an email away.
valerie@definingiam.com

What was the highlight of your week?

____

____

____

How did you manage your "Focus" for the week?

____

____

____

What were your top 2 Wins this week?

1. ______________________________
2. ______________________________

How did you complete this weeks challenge exercise?

____

____

____

Notes

"The truth will set you free, but only if you allow yourself to see it."

-WE by: Gillian Anderson & Jennifer Nadel

WEEK FIVE

Prepare Your Mind(set)

• • • • • • • • • • •

Truth Challenge

When it comes to facing the truth about who we are, how we feel and how we affect others, we often put our blinders on. You can't change what you don't address. This week, take off the blinders and reveal a truth you struggle with to someone you trust.

My personal focus for this week is ______________________________

____

____

____

____

____

My truth is ____

____

____

____

____

____

Date: ____/ ____/ 20____

Good Morning Sunshine!

Waking up with gratitude cultivates a positive attitude. Think thankful.

I am grateful for ____

____

It makes me happy when ____

____

The most important thing you can wear is your confidence. Affirm yourself.

I love you ______________________
Your Name

You ____

____

Change is inevitable but growth is by choice. Be intentional.

Today I challenge myself to ____

____

I proclaim that I ____

RECITE ALL OF THE ABOVE 3 TIMES OUT LOUD

How was your day?

Remember today you just made history. Celebrate you!

A great experience I had today was ___________________________________

____

Your future is counting on you to make the most of today. Be optimistic.

A challenge I had today was ____

____

A Win I had today was ____

____

I Dream of ____

SPEND 5 MINUTES MEDITATING ON YOUR DREAMS

Date: ____ / ____ / 20____

Good Morning Sunshine!

Waking up with gratitude cultivates a positive attitude. Think thankful.

I am grateful for ______________________________

____

It makes me happy when ______________________________

____

The most important thing you can wear is your confidence. Affirm yourself.

I love you ______________________________
Your Name

You ______________________________

____

Change is inevitable but growth is by choice. Be intentional.

Today I challenge myself to ______________________________

____

I proclaim that I ______________________________

RECITE ALL OF THE ABOVE 3 TIMES OUT LOUD

How was your day?

Remember today you just made history. Celebrate you!

A great experience I had today was ______________________________

____

Your future is counting on you to make the most of today. Be optimistic.

A challenge I had today was ______________________________

____

A Win I had today was ______________________________

____

I Dream of ______________________________

SPEND 5 MINUTES MEDITATING ON YOUR DREAMS

Date: ____/ ____/ 20____

Good Morning Sunshine!

Waking up with gratitude cultivates a positive attitude. Think thankful.

I am grateful for ______________________________

____

It makes me happy when ______________________________

____

The most important thing you can wear is your confidence. Affirm yourself.

I love you ______________________________
Your Name

You ______________________________

____

Change is inevitable but growth is by choice. Be intentional.

Today I challenge myself to ______________________________

____

I proclaim that I ______________________________

RECITE ALL OF THE ABOVE 3 TIMES OUT LOUD

How was your day?

Remember today you just made history. Celebrate you!

A great experience I had today was ______________________________

____

Your future is counting on you to make the most of today. Be optimistic.

A challenge I had today was ______________________________

____

A Win I had today was ______________________________

____

I Dream of ______________________________

SPEND 5 MINUTES MEDITATING ON YOUR DREAMS

Date: ____/ ____/ 20____

Good Morning Sunshine!

Waking up with gratitude cultivates a positive attitude. Think thankful.

I am grateful for ______________________________

____

It makes me happy when ______________________________

____

The most important thing you can wear is your confidence. Affirm yourself.

I love you ______________________________
Your Name

You ______________________________

____

Change is inevitable but growth is by choice. Be intentional.

Today I challenge myself to ______________________________

____

I proclaim that I ______________________________

RECITE ALL OF THE ABOVE 3 TIMES OUT LOUD

How was your day?

Remember today you just made history. Celebrate you!

A great experience I had today was ______________________________

____

Your future is counting on you to make the most of today. Be optimistic.

A challenge I had today was ______________________________

____

A Win I had today was ______________________________

____

I Dream of ______________________________

SPEND 5 MINUTES MEDITATING ON YOUR DREAMS

Date: ____/ ____/ 20____

Good Morning Sunshine!

Waking up with gratitude cultivates a positive attitude. Think thankful.

I am grateful for ____

____

It makes me happy when ____

____

The most important thing you can wear is your confidence. Affirm yourself.

I love you ____________________
Your Name

You ____

____

Change is inevitable but growth is by choice. Be intentional.

Today I challenge myself to _______________________________________

____

I proclaim that I ____

RECITE ALL OF THE ABOVE 3 TIMES OUT LOUD

How was your day?

Remember today you just made history. Celebrate you!

A great experience I had today was _________________________________

____

Your future is counting on you to make the most of today. Be optimistic.

A challenge I had today was _______________________________________

____

A Win I had today was ____

____

I Dream of ____

SPEND 5 MINUTES MEDITATING ON YOUR DREAMS

Date: ____/ ____/ 20____

Good Morning Sunshine!

Waking up with gratitude cultivates a positive attitude. Think thankful.

I am grateful for ______________________________

____

It makes me happy when ______________________________

____

The most important thing you can wear is your confidence. Affirm yourself.

I love you ______________________________
Your Name

You ______________________________

____

Change is inevitable but growth is by choice. Be intentional.

Today I challenge myself to ______________________________

____

I proclaim that I ______________________________

RECITE ALL OF THE ABOVE 3 TIMES OUT LOUD

How was your day?

Remember today you just made history. Celebrate you!

A great experience I had today was ______________________________

____

Your future is counting on you to make the most of today. Be optimistic.

A challenge I had today was ______________________________

____

A Win I had today was ______________________________

____

I Dream of ______________________________

SPEND 5 MINUTES MEDITATING ON YOUR DREAMS

Date: ____/ ____/ 20____

Good Morning Sunshine!

Waking up with gratitude cultivates a positive attitude. Think thankful.

I am grateful for ______________________________

____

It makes me happy when ______________________________

____

The most important thing you can wear is your confidence. Affirm yourself.

I love you ______________________________
Your Name

You ______________________________

____

Change is inevitable but growth is by choice. Be intentional.

Today I challenge myself to ______________________________

____

I proclaim that I ______________________________

RECITE ALL OF THE ABOVE 3 TIMES OUT LOUD

How was your day?

Remember today you just made history. Celebrate you!

A great experience I had today was ______________________________

____

Your future is counting on you to make the most of today. Be optimistic.

A challenge I had today was ______________________________

____

A Win I had today was ______________________________

____

I Dream of ______________________________

SPEND 5 MINUTES MEDITATING ON YOUR DREAMS

Weekly Recap

• • • • • • • • •

Don't forget to stop and smell the roses.
-Walter Hagen

Take a moment to reflect on this week's wins and challenges. If you need any personal coaching or guidance I'm only an email away.

valerie@definingiam.com

What was the highlight of your week?

____

____

____

How did you manage your "Focus" for the week?

____

____

____

What were your top 2 Wins this week?

1. ______________________________
2. ______________________________

How did you complete this weeks challenge exercise?

____

____

____

Notes

Letting go of the problem frees your hands to receive the solution.

ACCEPT WHAT IS.

WEEK SIX

Prepare Your Mind(set)

• • • • • • • • • • •

Acceptance Challenge

"Grant me the serenity to accept the things I cannot change, the courage to change the things I can, and the wisdom to know the difference," Reinhold Niebuhr. This week take some time to identify three problems that worry you the most. Determine whether it's something you can change or not. If you can, ACT. If not, accept it and let it goooo.

My personal focus for this week is ______________________________

____

____

____

____

____

The problems I need to access are ______________________________

____

____

____

____

____

Date: ____/ ____/ 20____

Good Morning Sunshine!

Waking up with gratitude cultivates a positive attitude. Think thankful.

I am grateful for ____________________

____

It makes me happy when ____________________

____

The most important thing you can wear is your confidence. Affirm yourself.

I love you ____________________
Your Name

You ____________________

____

Change is inevitable but growth is by choice. Be intentional.

Today I challenge myself to ____________________

____

I proclaim that I ____________________

RECITE ALL OF THE ABOVE 3 TIMES OUT LOUD

How was your day?

Remember today you just made history. Celebrate you!

A great experience I had today was ____________________

____

Your future is counting on you to make the most of today. Be optimistic.

A challenge I had today was ____________________

____

A Win I had today was ____________________

____

I Dream of ____________________

SPEND 5 MINUTES MEDITATING ON YOUR DREAMS

Date: ____ / ____ / 20____

Good Morning Sunshine!

Waking up with gratitude cultivates a positive attitude. Think thankful.

I am grateful for ____________________

____

It makes me happy when ____________________

____

The most important thing you can wear is your confidence. Affirm yourself.

I love you ____________________
Your Name

You ____________________

____

Change is inevitable but growth is by choice. Be intentional.

Today I challenge myself to ____________________

____

I proclaim that I ____________________

RECITE ALL OF THE ABOVE 3 TIMES OUT LOUD

How was your day?

Remember today you just made history. Celebrate you!

A great experience I had today was ____________________

____

Your future is counting on you to make the most of today. Be optimistic.

A challenge I had today was ____________________

____

A Win I had today was ____________________

____

I Dream of ____________________

SPEND 5 MINUTES MEDITATING ON YOUR DREAMS

Date: ____/ ____/ 20____

Good Morning Sunshine!

Waking up with gratitude cultivates a positive attitude. Think thankful.

I am grateful for ____

____

It makes me happy when ____

____

The most important thing you can wear is your confidence. Affirm yourself.

I love you ______________________
Your Name

You ____

____

Change is inevitable but growth is by choice. Be intentional.

Today I challenge myself to ____

____

I proclaim that I ____

RECITE ALL OF THE ABOVE 3 TIMES OUT LOUD

How was your day?

Remember today you just made history. Celebrate you!

A great experience I had today was ____

____

Your future is counting on you to make the most of today. Be optimistic.

A challenge I had today was ____

____

A Win I had today was ____

____

I Dream of ____

SPEND 5 MINUTES MEDITATING ON YOUR DREAMS

Date: ____ / ____ / 20____

Good Morning Sunshine!

Waking up with gratitude cultivates a positive attitude. Think thankful.

I am grateful for ______________________________

____

It makes me happy when ______________________________

____

The most important thing you can wear is your confidence. Affirm yourself.

I love you ______________________________
Your Name

You ______________________________

____

Change is inevitable but growth is by choice. Be intentional.

Today I challenge myself to ______________________________

____

I proclaim that I ______________________________

RECITE ALL OF THE ABOVE 3 TIMES OUT LOUD

How was your day?

Remember today you just made history. Celebrate you!

A great experience I had today was ______________________________

____

Your future is counting on you to make the most of today. Be optimistic.

A challenge I had today was ______________________________

____

A Win I had today was ______________________________

____

I Dream of ______________________________

SPEND 5 MINUTES MEDITATING ON YOUR DREAMS

Date: ____/ ____/ 20____

Good Morning Sunshine!

Waking up with gratitude cultivates a positive attitude. Think thankful.

I am grateful for ____

____

It makes me happy when ____

____

The most important thing you can wear is your confidence. Affirm yourself.

I love you ____________________
Your Name

You ____

____

Change is inevitable but growth is by choice. Be intentional.

Today I challenge myself to ____

____

I proclaim that I ____

RECITE ALL OF THE ABOVE 3 TIMES OUT LOUD

How was your day?

Remember today you just made history. Celebrate you!

A great experience I had today was ____

____

Your future is counting on you to make the most of today. Be optimistic.

A challenge I had today was ____

____

A Win I had today was ____

____

I Dream of ____

SPEND 5 MINUTES MEDITATING ON YOUR DREAMS

Date: ____/ ____/ 20____

Good Morning Sunshine!

Waking up with gratitude cultivates a positive attitude. Think thankful.

I am grateful for ____

____

It makes me happy when ____

____

The most important thing you can wear is your confidence. Affirm yourself.

I love you ________________________
Your Name

You ____

____

Change is inevitable but growth is by choice. Be intentional.

Today I challenge myself to ____

____

I proclaim that I ____

RECITE ALL OF THE ABOVE 3 TIMES OUT LOUD

How was your day?

Remember today you just made history. Celebrate you!

A great experience I had today was ____

____

Your future is counting on you to make the most of today. Be optimistic.

A challenge I had today was ____

____

A Win I had today was ____

____

I Dream of ____

SPEND 5 MINUTES MEDITATING ON YOUR DREAMS

Date: ____/ ____/ 20____

Good Morning Sunshine!

Waking up with gratitude cultivates a positive attitude. Think thankful.

I am grateful for ______________________________

____

It makes me happy when ______________________________

____

The most important thing you can wear is your confidence. Affirm yourself.

I love you ______________________________
Your Name

You ______________________________

____

Change is inevitable but growth is by choice. Be intentional.

Today I challenge myself to ______________________________

____

I proclaim that I ______________________________

RECITE ALL OF THE ABOVE 3 TIMES OUT LOUD

How was your day?

Remember today you just made history. Celebrate you!

A great experience I had today was ______________________________

____

Your future is counting on you to make the most of today. Be optimistic.

A challenge I had today was ______________________________

____

A Win I had today was ______________________________

____

I Dream of ______________________________

SPEND 5 MINUTES MEDITATING ON YOUR DREAMS

Weekly Recap

• • • • • • • • • •

Don't forget to stop and smell the roses.
-Walter Hagen

Take a moment to reflect on this week's wins and challenges. If you need any personal coaching or guidance I'm only an email away.

valerie@definingiam.com

What was the highlight of your week?

____

____

____

How did you manage your "Focus" for the week?

____

____

____

What were your top 2 Wins this week?

1. ______________________________
2. ______________________________

How did you complete this weeks challenge exercise?

____

____

____

Notes

I AM
Who I say
I AM.
I AM Defined
by ME.

BE YOU–UNAPOLOGETICALLY.

WEEK SEVEN

Prepare Your Mind(set)

• • • • • • • • • • •

I Am Challenge

Accept no one's definition of you. Define yourself for yourself. This week, get creative and create a fun name for yourself that describes who you are. Write it on a post-it, put it on your bathroom mirror, and say,

"Good Morning ___*Your New Name*___!"

My personal focus for this week is ______________________________

____

____

____

____

____

My new name is ______________________________________

____

____

____

____

____

Date: ____ / ____ / 20____

Good Morning Sunshine!

Waking up with gratitude cultivates a positive attitude. Think thankful.

I am grateful for ______________________________

____

It makes me happy when ______________________________

____

The most important thing you can wear is your confidence. Affirm yourself.

I love you ______________________________
Your Name

You ______________________________

____

Change is inevitable but growth is by choice. Be intentional.

Today I challenge myself to ______________________________

____

I proclaim that I ______________________________

RECITE ALL OF THE ABOVE 3 TIMES OUT LOUD

How was your day?

Remember today you just made history. Celebrate you!

A great experience I had today was ______________________________

____

Your future is counting on you to make the most of today. Be optimistic.

A challenge I had today was ______________________________

____

A Win I had today was ______________________________

____

I Dream of ______________________________

SPEND 5 MINUTES MEDITATING ON YOUR DREAMS

Date: ____/ ____/ 20____

Good Morning Sunshine!

Waking up with gratitude cultivates a positive attitude. Think thankful.

I am grateful for ______________________________

____

It makes me happy when ______________________________

____

The most important thing you can wear is your confidence. Affirm yourself.

I love you ______________________________
Your Name

You ______________________________

____

Change is inevitable but growth is by choice. Be intentional.

Today I challenge myself to ______________________________

____

I proclaim that I ______________________________

RECITE ALL OF THE ABOVE 3 TIMES OUT LOUD

How was your day?

Remember today you just made history. Celebrate you!

A great experience I had today was ______________________________

____

Your future is counting on you to make the most of today. Be optimistic.

A challenge I had today was ______________________________

____

A Win I had today was ______________________________

____

I Dream of ______________________________

SPEND 5 MINUTES MEDITATING ON YOUR DREAMS

Date: ____/ ____/ 20____

Good Morning Sunshine!

Waking up with gratitude cultivates a positive attitude. Think thankful.

I am grateful for ____

____

It makes me happy when ____

____

The most important thing you can wear is your confidence. Affirm yourself.

I love you ______________________
Your Name

You ____

____

Change is inevitable but growth is by choice. Be intentional.

Today I challenge myself to ____

____

I proclaim that I ____

RECITE ALL OF THE ABOVE 3 TIMES OUT LOUD

How was your day?

Remember today you just made history. Celebrate you!

A great experience I had today was ___________________________________

____

Your future is counting on you to make the most of today. Be optimistic.

A challenge I had today was ____

____

A Win I had today was ____

____

I Dream of ____

SPEND 5 MINUTES MEDITATING ON YOUR DREAMS

Date: ____/ ____/ 20____

Good Morning Sunshine!

Waking up with gratitude cultivates a positive attitude. Think thankful.

I am grateful for ______________________________

____

It makes me happy when ______________________________

____

The most important thing you can wear is your confidence. Affirm yourself.

I love you ______________________________
Your Name

You ______________________________

____

Change is inevitable but growth is by choice. Be intentional.

Today I challenge myself to ______________________________

____

I proclaim that I ______________________________

RECITE ALL OF THE ABOVE 3 TIMES OUT LOUD

How was your day?

Remember today you just made history. Celebrate you!

A great experience I had today was ______________________________

____

Your future is counting on you to make the most of today. Be optimistic.

A challenge I had today was ______________________________

____

A Win I had today was ______________________________

____

I Dream of ______________________________

SPEND 5 MINUTES MEDITATING ON YOUR DREAMS

Date: ____ / ____ / 20____

Good Morning Sunshine!

Waking up with gratitude cultivates a positive attitude. Think thankful.

I am grateful for ______________________________

____

It makes me happy when ______________________________

____

The most important thing you can wear is your confidence. Affirm yourself.

I love you ______________________________
Your Name

You ______________________________

____

Change is inevitable but growth is by choice. Be intentional.

Today I challenge myself to ______________________________

____

I proclaim that I ______________________________

RECITE ALL OF THE ABOVE 3 TIMES OUT LOUD

How was your day?

Remember today you just made history. Celebrate you!

A great experience I had today was ______________________________

____

Your future is counting on you to make the most of today. Be optimistic.

A challenge I had today was ______________________________

____

A Win I had today was ______________________________

____

I Dream of ______________________________

SPEND 5 MINUTES MEDITATING ON YOUR DREAMS

Date: ____/ ____/ 20____

Good Morning Sunshine!

Waking up with gratitude cultivates a positive attitude. Think thankful.

I am grateful for ____

____

It makes me happy when ____

____

The most important thing you can wear is your confidence. Affirm yourself.

I love you ________________________
Your Name

You ____

____

Change is inevitable but growth is by choice. Be intentional.

Today I challenge myself to ____

____

I proclaim that I ____

RECITE ALL OF THE ABOVE 3 TIMES OUT LOUD

How was your day?

Remember today you just made history. Celebrate you!

A great experience I had today was ____

____

Your future is counting on you to make the most of today. Be optimistic.

A challenge I had today was ____

____

A Win I had today was ____

____

I Dream of ____

SPEND 5 MINUTES MEDITATING ON YOUR DREAMS

Date: ____ / ____ / 20____

Good Morning Sunshine!

Waking up with gratitude cultivates a positive attitude. Think thankful.

I am grateful for ____

____

It makes me happy when ____

____

The most important thing you can wear is your confidence. Affirm yourself.

I love you ____________________
Your Name

You ____

____

Change is inevitable but growth is by choice. Be intentional.

Today I challenge myself to ____

____

I proclaim that I ____

RECITE ALL OF THE ABOVE 3 TIMES OUT LOUD

How was your day?

Remember today you just made history. Celebrate you!

A great experience I had today was ____

____

Your future is counting on you to make the most of today. Be optimistic.

A challenge I had today was ____

____

A Win I had today was ____

____

I Dream of ____

SPEND 5 MINUTES MEDITATING ON YOUR DREAMS

Weekly Recap

• • • • • • • • •

Don't forget to stop and smell the roses.
-Walter Hagen

Take a moment to reflect on this week's wins and challenges. If you need any personal coaching or guidance I'm only an email away.

valerie@definingiam.com

What was the highlight of your week?

____

____

____

How did you manage your "Focus" for the week?

____

____

____

What were your top 2 Wins this week?

1. ____
2. ____

How did you complete this weeks challenge exercise?

____

____

____

Notes

Don't run from fear. Instead let it push you to win the race.

FACING YOUR FEARS IS AN AUTOMATIC WIN.

WEEK EIGHT

Prepare Your Mind(set)

• • • • • • • • • • •

Fear Challenge

Fear's purpose is not to hold you back. Its really designed to show you where your strength lies and pave the way to your best life. But all too often we give fear a bad rap. The minute it peaks its little head, we run like we saw a ghost. So, you've guessed it, this week do one thing that scares the crap out of you. Then celebrate your growth on the other side.

My personal focus for this week is ________________________________

____

____

____

____

____

The fear I am going to face is ________________________________

____

____

____

____

____

Date: ____/ ____/ 20____

Good Morning Sunshine!

Waking up with gratitude cultivates a positive attitude. Think thankful.

I am grateful for ______________________________

____

It makes me happy when ______________________________

____

The most important thing you can wear is your confidence. Affirm yourself.

I love you ______________________________
Your Name

You ______________________________

____

Change is inevitable but growth is by choice. Be intentional.

Today I challenge myself to ______________________________

____

I proclaim that I ______________________________

RECITE ALL OF THE ABOVE 3 TIMES OUT LOUD

How was your day?

Remember today you just made history. Celebrate you!

A great experience I had today was ______________________________

____

Your future is counting on you to make the most of today. Be optimistic.

A challenge I had today was ______________________________

____

A Win I had today was ______________________________

____

I Dream of ______________________________

SPEND 5 MINUTES MEDITATING ON YOUR DREAMS

Date: ____/ ____/ 20____

Good Morning Sunshine!

Waking up with gratitude cultivates a positive attitude. Think thankful.

I am grateful for ____

____

It makes me happy when ____

____

The most important thing you can wear is your confidence. Affirm yourself.

I love you ______________________
Your Name

You ____

____

Change is inevitable but growth is by choice. Be intentional.

Today I challenge myself to ____

____

I proclaim that I ____

RECITE ALL OF THE ABOVE 3 TIMES OUT LOUD

How was your day?

Remember today you just made history. Celebrate you!

A great experience I had today was ____

____

Your future is counting on you to make the most of today. Be optimistic.

A challenge I had today was ____

____

A Win I had today was ____

____

I Dream of ____

SPEND 5 MINUTES MEDITATING ON YOUR DREAMS

Date: ____/ ____/ 20____

Good Morning Sunshine!

Waking up with gratitude cultivates a positive attitude. Think thankful.

I am grateful for ______________________________

____

It makes me happy when ______________________________

____

The most important thing you can wear is your confidence. Affirm yourself.

I love you ______________________________
Your Name

You ______________________________

____

Change is inevitable but growth is by choice. Be intentional.

Today I challenge myself to ______________________________

____

I proclaim that I ______________________________

RECITE ALL OF THE ABOVE 3 TIMES OUT LOUD

How was your day?

Remember today you just made history. Celebrate you!

A great experience I had today was ______________________________

____

Your future is counting on you to make the most of today. Be optimistic.

A challenge I had today was ______________________________

____

A Win I had today was ______________________________

____

I Dream of ______________________________

SPEND 5 MINUTES MEDITATING ON YOUR DREAMS

Date: ____/ ____/ 20____

Good Morning Sunshine!

Waking up with gratitude cultivates a positive attitude. Think thankful.

I am grateful for ____

____

It makes me happy when ____

____

The most important thing you can wear is your confidence. Affirm yourself.

I love you ____________________
Your Name

You ____

____

Change is inevitable but growth is by choice. Be intentional.

Today I challenge myself to ____

____

I proclaim that I ____

RECITE ALL OF THE ABOVE 3 TIMES OUT LOUD

How was your day?

Remember today you just made history. Celebrate you!

A great experience I had today was ____

____

Your future is counting on you to make the most of today. Be optimistic.

A challenge I had today was ____

____

A Win I had today was ____

____

I Dream of ____

SPEND 5 MINUTES MEDITATING ON YOUR DREAMS

Date: ____/ ____/ 20____

Good Morning Sunshine!

Waking up with gratitude cultivates a positive attitude. Think thankful.

I am grateful for ______________________________

____

It makes me happy when ______________________________

____

The most important thing you can wear is your confidence. Affirm yourself.

I love you ______________________________
Your Name

You ______________________________

____

Change is inevitable but growth is by choice. Be intentional.

Today I challenge myself to ______________________________

____

I proclaim that I ______________________________

RECITE ALL OF THE ABOVE 3 TIMES OUT LOUD

How was your day?

Remember today you just made history. Celebrate you!

A great experience I had today was ______________________________

____

Your future is counting on you to make the most of today. Be optimistic.

A challenge I had today was ______________________________

____

A Win I had today was ______________________________

____

I Dream of ______________________________

SPEND 5 MINUTES MEDITATING ON YOUR DREAMS

Date: ____/ ____/ 20____

Good Morning Sunshine!

Waking up with gratitude cultivates a positive attitude. Think thankful.

I am grateful for ____

____

It makes me happy when ____

____

The most important thing you can wear is your confidence. Affirm yourself.

I love you ______________________
Your Name

You ____

____

Change is inevitable but growth is by choice. Be intentional.

Today I challenge myself to ____

____

I proclaim that I ____

RECITE ALL OF THE ABOVE 3 TIMES OUT LOUD

How was your day?

Remember today you just made history. Celebrate you!

A great experience I had today was ____

____

Your future is counting on you to make the most of today. Be optimistic.

A challenge I had today was ____

____

A Win I had today was ____

____

I Dream of ____

SPEND 5 MINUTES MEDITATING ON YOUR DREAMS

Date: ____/ ____/ 20____

Good Morning Sunshine!

Waking up with gratitude cultivates a positive attitude. Think thankful.

I am grateful for ________________________________

____

It makes me happy when ________________________________

____

The most important thing you can wear is your confidence. Affirm yourself.

I love you ________________________________
Your Name

You ________________________________

____

Change is inevitable but growth is by choice. Be intentional.

Today I challenge myself to ________________________________

____

I proclaim that I ________________________________

RECITE ALL OF THE ABOVE 3 TIMES OUT LOUD

How was your day?

Remember today you just made history. Celebrate you!

A great experience I had today was ________________________________

____

Your future is counting on you to make the most of today. Be optimistic.

A challenge I had today was ________________________________

____

A Win I had today was ________________________________

____

I Dream of ________________________________

SPEND 5 MINUTES MEDITATING ON YOUR DREAMS

Weekly Recap

• • • • • • • • • •

Don't forget to stop and smell the roses.
-Walter Hagen

Take a moment to reflect on this week's wins and challenges. If you need any personal coaching or guidance I'm only an email away.

valerie@definingiam.com

What was the highlight of your week?

____

____

____

How did you manage your "Focus" for the week?

____

____

____

What were your top 2 Wins this week?

1. ____
2. ____

How did you complete this weeks challenge exercise?

____

____

____

Notes

The greatest disappointments in life come from unmet expectations.

CHECK WHAT YOU EXPECT.

WEEK NINE

Prepare Your Mind(set)

• • • • • • • • • • •

Expectations Challenge

The problem with expectations is not that we have them, it's that we don't know how to handle the disappointment of them not being met. Our expectations often carry hidden beliefs about ourselves, which scream bloody murder when disappointment exposes them. Address the belief, not the expectation. What are three beliefs that drive your expectations?

My personal focus for this week is ______________________________

____

____

____

____

____

The beliefs I need to address are ______________________________

____

____

____

____

____

Date: ____/ ____/ 20____

Good Morning Sunshine!

Waking up with gratitude cultivates a positive attitude. Think thankful.

I am grateful for ______________________________

____

It makes me happy when ______________________________

____

The most important thing you can wear is your confidence. Affirm yourself.

I love you ______________________________
Your Name

You ______________________________

____

Change is inevitable but growth is by choice. Be intentional.

Today I challenge myself to ______________________________

____

I proclaim that I ______________________________

RECITE ALL OF THE ABOVE 3 TIMES OUT LOUD

How was your day?

Remember today you just made history. Celebrate you!

A great experience I had today was ______________________________

____

Your future is counting on you to make the most of today. Be optimistic.

A challenge I had today was ______________________________

____

A Win I had today was ______________________________

____

I Dream of ______________________________

SPEND 5 MINUTES MEDITATING ON YOUR DREAMS

Date: ____/ ____/ 20____

Good Morning Sunshine!

Waking up with gratitude cultivates a positive attitude. Think thankful.

I am grateful for ______________________________

____

It makes me happy when ______________________________

____

The most important thing you can wear is your confidence. Affirm yourself.

I love you ______________________________
Your Name

You ______________________________

____

Change is inevitable but growth is by choice. Be intentional.

Today I challenge myself to ______________________________

____

I proclaim that I ______________________________

RECITE ALL OF THE ABOVE 3 TIMES OUT LOUD

How was your day?

Remember today you just made history. Celebrate you!

A great experience I had today was ______________________________

____

Your future is counting on you to make the most of today. Be optimistic.

A challenge I had today was ______________________________

____

A Win I had today was ______________________________

____

I Dream of ______________________________

SPEND 5 MINUTES MEDITATING ON YOUR DREAMS

Date: ____/ ____/ 20____

Good Morning Sunshine!

Waking up with gratitude cultivates a positive attitude. Think thankful.

I am grateful for ____

____

It makes me happy when ____

____

The most important thing you can wear is your confidence. Affirm yourself.

I love you ______________________
Your Name

You ____

____

Change is inevitable but growth is by choice. Be intentional.

Today I challenge myself to ____

____

I proclaim that I ____

RECITE ALL OF THE ABOVE 3 TIMES OUT LOUD

How was your day?

Remember today you just made history. Celebrate you!

A great experience I had today was ____

____

Your future is counting on you to make the most of today. Be optimistic.

A challenge I had today was ____

____

A Win I had today was ____

____

I Dream of ____

SPEND 5 MINUTES MEDITATING ON YOUR DREAMS

Date: ____/ ____/ 20____

Good Morning Sunshine!

Waking up with gratitude cultivates a positive attitude. Think thankful.

I am grateful for ______________________________

____

It makes me happy when ______________________________

____

The most important thing you can wear is your confidence. Affirm yourself.

I love you ______________________________
Your Name

You ______________________________

____

Change is inevitable but growth is by choice. Be intentional.

Today I challenge myself to ______________________________

____

I proclaim that I ______________________________

RECITE ALL OF THE ABOVE 3 TIMES OUT LOUD

How was your day?

Remember today you just made history. Celebrate you!

A great experience I had today was ______________________________

____

Your future is counting on you to make the most of today. Be optimistic.

A challenge I had today was ______________________________

____

A Win I had today was ______________________________

____

I Dream of ______________________________

SPEND 5 MINUTES MEDITATING ON YOUR DREAMS

Date: ____/ ____/ 20____

Good Morning Sunshine!

Waking up with gratitude cultivates a positive attitude. Think thankful.

I am grateful for ____

____

It makes me happy when ____

____

The most important thing you can wear is your confidence. Affirm yourself.

I love you ______________________________
Your Name

You ____

____

Change is inevitable but growth is by choice. Be intentional.

Today I challenge myself to ____

____

I proclaim that I ____

RECITE ALL OF THE ABOVE 3 TIMES OUT LOUD

How was your day?

Remember today you just made history. Celebrate you!

A great experience I had today was ____

____

Your future is counting on you to make the most of today. Be optimistic.

A challenge I had today was ____

____

A Win I had today was ____

____

I Dream of ____

SPEND 5 MINUTES MEDITATING ON YOUR DREAMS

Date: ____/ ____/ 20____

Good Morning Sunshine!

Waking up with gratitude cultivates a positive attitude. Think thankful.

I am grateful for ______________________________

____

It makes me happy when ______________________________

____

The most important thing you can wear is your confidence. Affirm yourself.

I love you ______________________________
Your Name

You ______________________________

____

Change is inevitable but growth is by choice. Be intentional.

Today I challenge myself to ______________________________

____

I proclaim that I ______________________________

RECITE ALL OF THE ABOVE 3 TIMES OUT LOUD

How was your day?

Remember today you just made history. Celebrate you!

A great experience I had today was ______________________________

____

Your future is counting on you to make the most of today. Be optimistic.

A challenge I had today was ______________________________

____

A Win I had today was ______________________________

____

I Dream of ______________________________

SPEND 5 MINUTES MEDITATING ON YOUR DREAMS

Date: ____/ ____/ 20____

Good Morning Sunshine!

Waking up with gratitude cultivates a positive attitude. Think thankful.

I am grateful for ____

____

It makes me happy when ____

____

The most important thing you can wear is your confidence. Affirm yourself.

I love you ____________________
Your Name

You ____

____

Change is inevitable but growth is by choice. Be intentional.

Today I challenge myself to ____

____

I proclaim that I ____

RECITE ALL OF THE ABOVE 3 TIMES OUT LOUD

How was your day?

Remember today you just made history. Celebrate you!

A great experience I had today was ____

____

Your future is counting on you to make the most of today. Be optimistic.

A challenge I had today was ____

____

A Win I had today was ____

____

I Dream of ____

SPEND 5 MINUTES MEDITATING ON YOUR DREAMS

Weekly Recap

• • • • • • • • • •

Don't forget to stop and smell the roses.
-Walter Hagen

Take a moment to reflect on this week's wins and challenges. If you need any personal coaching or guidance I'm only an email away.
valerie@definingiam.com

What was the highlight of your week?

____

____

____

How did you manage your "Focus" for the week?

____

____

____

What were your top 2 Wins this week?

1. ____
2. ____

How did you complete this weeks challenge exercise?

____

____

____

Notes

Your life is the sum of the things you do, not what you say you're going to do.

TO DO OR NOT TO DO, THAT IS THE QUESTION.

WEEK TEN

Prepare Your Mind(set)

• • • • • • • • • • •

Decision Challenge

If I asked you to tell me about your life, would you tell me about the things you've done or the things you thought about doing? Exactly my point. Don't talk about it, be about it. It's really as simple as that. Doing starts with a decision, and decisions are non-negotiable. Pick one thing you said you were going to do and commit to doing it this week.

My personal focus for this week is ______________________________

____

____

____

____

____

This week I will ____

____

____

____

____

____

Date: ____/ ____/ 20____

Good Morning Sunshine!

Waking up with gratitude cultivates a positive attitude. Think thankful.

I am grateful for ______________________________

____

It makes me happy when ______________________________

____

The most important thing you can wear is your confidence. Affirm yourself.

I love you ______________________________
Your Name

You ______________________________

____

Change is inevitable but growth is by choice. Be intentional.

Today I challenge myself to ______________________________

____

I proclaim that I ______________________________

RECITE ALL OF THE ABOVE 3 TIMES OUT LOUD

How was your day?

Remember today you just made history. Celebrate you!

A great experience I had today was ______________________________

____

Your future is counting on you to make the most of today. Be optimistic.

A challenge I had today was ______________________________

____

A Win I had today was ______________________________

____

I Dream of ______________________________

SPEND 5 MINUTES MEDITATING ON YOUR DREAMS

Date: ____ / ____ / 20____

Good Morning Sunshine!

Waking up with gratitude cultivates a positive attitude. Think thankful.

I am grateful for ____

____

It makes me happy when ____________________________________

____

The most important thing you can wear is your confidence. Affirm yourself.

I love you ____________________
Your Name

You ____

____

Change is inevitable but growth is by choice. Be intentional.

Today I challenge myself to __________________________________

____

I proclaim that I ____

RECITE ALL OF THE ABOVE 3 TIMES OUT LOUD

How was your day?

Remember today you just made history. Celebrate you!

A great experience I had today was ____________________________

____

Your future is counting on you to make the most of today. Be optimistic.

A challenge I had today was ________________________________

____

A Win I had today was ____________________________________

____

I Dream of ____

SPEND 5 MINUTES MEDITATING ON YOUR DREAMS

Date: ____/ ____/ 20____

Good Morning Sunshine!

Waking up with gratitude cultivates a positive attitude. Think thankful.

I am grateful for ____

____

It makes me happy when ____

____

The most important thing you can wear is your confidence. Affirm yourself.

I love you ______________________
Your Name

You ____

____

Change is inevitable but growth is by choice. Be intentional.

Today I challenge myself to ____

____

I proclaim that I ____

RECITE ALL OF THE ABOVE 3 TIMES OUT LOUD

How was your day?

Remember today you just made history. Celebrate you!

A great experience I had today was ____

____

Your future is counting on you to make the most of today. Be optimistic.

A challenge I had today was ____

____

A Win I had today was ____

____

I Dream of ____

SPEND 5 MINUTES MEDITATING ON YOUR DREAMS

Date: ____/ ____/ 20____

Good Morning Sunshine!

Waking up with gratitude cultivates a positive attitude. Think thankful.

I am grateful for ______________________________

____

It makes me happy when ______________________________

____

The most important thing you can wear is your confidence. Affirm yourself.

I love you ______________________________
Your Name

You ______________________________

____

Change is inevitable but growth is by choice. Be intentional.

Today I challenge myself to ______________________________

____

I proclaim that I ______________________________

RECITE ALL OF THE ABOVE 3 TIMES OUT LOUD

How was your day?

Remember today you just made history. Celebrate you!

A great experience I had today was ______________________________

____

Your future is counting on you to make the most of today. Be optimistic.

A challenge I had today was ______________________________

____

A Win I had today was ______________________________

____

I Dream of ______________________________

SPEND 5 MINUTES MEDITATING ON YOUR DREAMS

Date: ____/ ____/ 20____

Good Morning Sunshine!

Waking up with gratitude cultivates a positive attitude. Think thankful.

I am grateful for ____

____

It makes me happy when ____

____

The most important thing you can wear is your confidence. Affirm yourself.

I love you ______________________
Your Name

You ____

____

Change is inevitable but growth is by choice. Be intentional.

Today I challenge myself to ____

____

I proclaim that I ____

RECITE ALL OF THE ABOVE 3 TIMES OUT LOUD

How was your day?

Remember today you just made history. Celebrate you!

A great experience I had today was ____

____

Your future is counting on you to make the most of today. Be optimistic.

A challenge I had today was ____

____

A Win I had today was ____

____

I Dream of ____

SPEND 5 MINUTES MEDITATING ON YOUR DREAMS

Date: ____ / ____ / 20____

Good Morning Sunshine!

Waking up with gratitude cultivates a positive attitude. Think thankful.

I am grateful for ______________________________

____

It makes me happy when ______________________________

____

The most important thing you can wear is your confidence. Affirm yourself.

I love you ______________________________
Your Name

You ______________________________

____

Change is inevitable but growth is by choice. Be intentional.

Today I challenge myself to ______________________________

____

I proclaim that I ______________________________

RECITE ALL OF THE ABOVE 3 TIMES OUT LOUD

How was your day?

Remember today you just made history. Celebrate you!

A great experience I had today was ______________________________

____

Your future is counting on you to make the most of today. Be optimistic.

A challenge I had today was ______________________________

____

A Win I had today was ______________________________

____

I Dream of ______________________________

SPEND 5 MINUTES MEDITATING ON YOUR DREAMS

Date: ____/ ____/ 20____

Good Morning Sunshine!

Waking up with gratitude cultivates a positive attitude. Think thankful.

I am grateful for ______________________________

____

It makes me happy when ______________________________

____

The most important thing you can wear is your confidence. Affirm yourself.

I love you ______________________________
Your Name

You ______________________________

____

Change is inevitable but growth is by choice. Be intentional.

Today I challenge myself to ______________________________

____

I proclaim that I ______________________________

RECITE ALL OF THE ABOVE 3 TIMES OUT LOUD

How was your day?

Remember today you just made history. Celebrate you!

A great experience I had today was ______________________________

____

Your future is counting on you to make the most of today. Be optimistic.

A challenge I had today was ______________________________

____

A Win I had today was ______________________________

____

I Dream of ______________________________

SPEND 5 MINUTES MEDITATING ON YOUR DREAMS

Weekly Recap

• • • • • • • • • •

Don't forget to stop and smell the roses.
-Walter Hagen

Take a moment to reflect on this week's wins and challenges. If you need any personal coaching or guidance I'm only an email away.

valerie@definingiam.com

What was the highlight of your week?

____

____

____

How did you manage your "Focus" for the week?

____

____

____

What were your top 2 Wins this week?

1. ______________________________
2. ______________________________

How did you complete this weeks challenge exercise?

____

____

____

Notes

"Allow yourself to go for what you want, not just what you think you can get."

-Self Love Experiment, Shannon Kaiser

WEEK ELEVEN

Prepare Your Mind(set)

• • • • • • • • • • •

Dream Challenge

Are your dreams only as big as your ability to make them happen? If so, I hate to tell you-you aren't dreaming, you are just making a to-do list. Dreams are supposed to seem bigger than your abilities so they can stretch you. This week, write down something that seems unrealistic for you to do or have in life and dream about it at least once a day.

My personal focus for this week is ____________________

My dream is ____________________

Date: ____/ ____/ 20____

Good Morning Sunshine!

Waking up with gratitude cultivates a positive attitude. Think thankful.

I am grateful for ____

____

It makes me happy when ____

____

The most important thing you can wear is your confidence. Affirm yourself.

I love you ____________________
Your Name

You ____

____

Change is inevitable but growth is by choice. Be intentional.

Today I challenge myself to ____

____

I proclaim that I ____

RECITE ALL OF THE ABOVE 3 TIMES OUT LOUD

How was your day?

Remember today you just made history. Celebrate you!

A great experience I had today was ____

____

Your future is counting on you to make the most of today. Be optimistic.

A challenge I had today was ____

____

A Win I had today was ____

____

I Dream of ____

SPEND 5 MINUTES MEDITATING ON YOUR DREAMS

Date: ____ / ____ / 20____

Good Morning Sunshine!

Waking up with gratitude cultivates a positive attitude. Think thankful.

I am grateful for ______________________________

____

It makes me happy when ______________________________

____

The most important thing you can wear is your confidence. Affirm yourself.

I love you ______________________________
Your Name

You ______________________________

____

Change is inevitable but growth is by choice. Be intentional.

Today I challenge myself to ______________________________

____

I proclaim that I ______________________________

RECITE ALL OF THE ABOVE 3 TIMES OUT LOUD

How was your day?

Remember today you just made history. Celebrate you!

A great experience I had today was ______________________________

____

Your future is counting on you to make the most of today. Be optimistic.

A challenge I had today was ______________________________

____

A Win I had today was ______________________________

____

I Dream of ______________________________

SPEND 5 MINUTES MEDITATING ON YOUR DREAMS

Date: ____/ ____/ 20____

Good Morning Sunshine!

Waking up with gratitude cultivates a positive attitude. Think thankful.

I am grateful for ______________________________

____

It makes me happy when ______________________________

____

The most important thing you can wear is your confidence. Affirm yourself.

I love you ______________________________
Your Name

You ______________________________

____

Change is inevitable but growth is by choice. Be intentional.

Today I challenge myself to ______________________________

____

I proclaim that I ______________________________

RECITE ALL OF THE ABOVE 3 TIMES OUT LOUD

How was your day?

Remember today you just made history. Celebrate you!

A great experience I had today was ______________________________

____

Your future is counting on you to make the most of today. Be optimistic.

A challenge I had today was ______________________________

____

A Win I had today was ______________________________

____

I Dream of ______________________________

SPEND 5 MINUTES MEDITATING ON YOUR DREAMS

Date: ____/ ____/ 20____

Good Morning Sunshine!

Waking up with gratitude cultivates a positive attitude. Think thankful.

I am grateful for ______________________________

____

It makes me happy when ______________________________

____

The most important thing you can wear is your confidence. Affirm yourself.

I love you ______________________________
Your Name

You ______________________________

____

Change is inevitable but growth is by choice. Be intentional.

Today I challenge myself to ______________________________

____

I proclaim that I ______________________________

RECITE ALL OF THE ABOVE 3 TIMES OUT LOUD

How was your day?

Remember today you just made history. Celebrate you!

A great experience I had today was ______________________________

____

Your future is counting on you to make the most of today. Be optimistic.

A challenge I had today was ______________________________

____

A Win I had today was ______________________________

____

I Dream of ______________________________

SPEND 5 MINUTES MEDITATING ON YOUR DREAMS

Date: ____/ ____/ 20____

Good Morning Sunshine!

Waking up with gratitude cultivates a positive attitude. Think thankful.

I am grateful for ____________________

____

It makes me happy when ____________________

____

The most important thing you can wear is your confidence. Affirm yourself.

I love you ____________________
Your Name

You ____________________

____

Change is inevitable but growth is by choice. Be intentional.

Today I challenge myself to ____________________

____

I proclaim that I ____________________

RECITE ALL OF THE ABOVE 3 TIMES OUT LOUD

How was your day?

Remember today you just made history. Celebrate you!

A great experience I had today was ____________________

____

Your future is counting on you to make the most of today. Be optimistic.

A challenge I had today was ____________________

____

A Win I had today was ____________________

____

I Dream of ____________________

SPEND 5 MINUTES MEDITATING ON YOUR DREAMS

Date: ____/ ____/ 20____

Good Morning Sunshine!

Waking up with gratitude cultivates a positive attitude. Think thankful.

I am grateful for ______________________________

____

It makes me happy when ______________________________

____

The most important thing you can wear is your confidence. Affirm yourself.

I love you ______________________________
Your Name

You ______________________________

____

Change is inevitable but growth is by choice. Be intentional.

Today I challenge myself to ______________________________

____

I proclaim that I ______________________________

RECITE ALL OF THE ABOVE 3 TIMES OUT LOUD

How was your day?

Remember today you just made history. Celebrate you!

A great experience I had today was ______________________________

____

Your future is counting on you to make the most of today. Be optimistic.

A challenge I had today was ______________________________

____

A Win I had today was ______________________________

____

I Dream of ______________________________

SPEND 5 MINUTES MEDITATING ON YOUR DREAMS

Date: ____/ ____/ 20____

Good Morning Sunshine!

Waking up with gratitude cultivates a positive attitude. Think thankful.

I am grateful for ______________________________

____

It makes me happy when ______________________________

____

The most important thing you can wear is your confidence. Affirm yourself.

I love you ______________________________
Your Name

You ______________________________

____

Change is inevitable but growth is by choice. Be intentional.

Today I challenge myself to ______________________________

____

I proclaim that I ______________________________

RECITE ALL OF THE ABOVE 3 TIMES OUT LOUD

How was your day?

Remember today you just made history. Celebrate you!

A great experience I had today was ______________________________

____

Your future is counting on you to make the most of today. Be optimistic.

A challenge I had today was ______________________________

____

A Win I had today was ______________________________

____

I Dream of ______________________________

SPEND 5 MINUTES MEDITATING ON YOUR DREAMS

Weekly Recap

• • • • • • • • •

Don't forget to stop and smell the roses.
-Walter Hagen

Take a moment to reflect on this week's wins and challenges. If you need any personal coaching or guidance I'm only an email away.

valerie@definingiam.com

What was the highlight of your week?

____

____

____

How did you manage your "Focus" for the week?

____

____

____

What were your top 2 Wins this week?

1. ____
2. ____

How did you complete this weeks challenge exercise?

____

____

____

Notes

Be Proactive Not Reactive

CHOOSE HOW YOU ACT.

Time to Reorder

• • • • • • • • • • •

Kudos to you! You are one week shy of completing your first 12 weeks of **The DEFINING I AM Journal**. At this point, I hope you can say you have gotten into your groove and are seeing some personal growth more and more each day. Remember you are on an ever-evolving journey that doesn't end after 12 weeks. Keep it going, and order your next 12-week journal today.

You owe it to yourself to do the best for yourself.

www.definingiam.com

KEEP GROWING!

Be the reason you smile today.

LOVE YOURSELF.

WEEK TWELVE

Prepare Your Mind(set)

• • • • • • • • • • •

Kindness Challenge

We grew up being told to "be nice" ever since the first time we clutched a toy and screamed, "Mine!" We were taught it's important to be kind to others, but somehow the part about being kind and loving to ourselves was left out. Don't underestimate the impact of a kind gesture. This week, treat yourself to an act of kindness you might otherwise do for someone else.

My personal focus for this week is ______________________________

I will be kind to myself by ______________________________

Date: ____/ ____/ 20____

Good Morning Sunshine!

Waking up with gratitude cultivates a positive attitude. Think thankful.

I am grateful for ______________________________

____

It makes me happy when ______________________________

____

The most important thing you can wear is your confidence. Affirm yourself.

I love you ______________________________
Your Name

You ______________________________

____

Change is inevitable but growth is by choice. Be intentional.

Today I challenge myself to ______________________________

____

I proclaim that I ______________________________

RECITE ALL OF THE ABOVE 3 TIMES OUT LOUD

How was your day?

Remember today you just made history. Celebrate you!

A great experience I had today was ______________________________

____

Your future is counting on you to make the most of today. Be optimistic.

A challenge I had today was ______________________________

____

A Win I had today was ______________________________

____

I Dream of ______________________________

SPEND 5 MINUTES MEDITATING ON YOUR DREAMS

Date: ____/ ____/ 20____

Good Morning Sunshine!

Waking up with gratitude cultivates a positive attitude. Think thankful.

I am grateful for ________________________________

____

It makes me happy when ________________________________

____

The most important thing you can wear is your confidence. Affirm yourself.

I love you ________________
Your Name

You ________________________________

____

Change is inevitable but growth is by choice. Be intentional.

Today I challenge myself to ________________________________

____

I proclaim that I ________________________________

RECITE ALL OF THE ABOVE 3 TIMES OUT LOUD

How was your day?

Remember today you just made history. Celebrate you!

A great experience I had today was ________________________________

____

Your future is counting on you to make the most of today. Be optimistic.

A challenge I had today was ________________________________

____

A Win I had today was ________________________________

____

I Dream of ________________________________

SPEND 5 MINUTES MEDITATING ON YOUR DREAMS

Date: ____/ ____/ 20____

Good Morning Sunshine!

Waking up with gratitude cultivates a positive attitude. Think thankful.

I am grateful for ____________________

____

It makes me happy when ____________________

____

The most important thing you can wear is your confidence. Affirm yourself.

I love you ____________________
Your Name

You ____________________

____

Change is inevitable but growth is by choice. Be intentional.

Today I challenge myself to ____________________

____

I proclaim that I ____________________

RECITE ALL OF THE ABOVE 3 TIMES OUT LOUD

How was your day?

Remember today you just made history. Celebrate you!

A great experience I had today was ____________________

____

Your future is counting on you to make the most of today. Be optimistic.

A challenge I had today was ____________________

____

A Win I had today was ____________________

____

I Dream of ____________________

SPEND 5 MINUTES MEDITATING ON YOUR DREAMS

Date: ____ / ____ / 20____

Good Morning Sunshine!

Waking up with gratitude cultivates a positive attitude. Think thankful.

I am grateful for ____

____

It makes me happy when ____

____

The most important thing you can wear is your confidence. Affirm yourself.

I love you ______________________
Your Name

You ____

____

Change is inevitable but growth is by choice. Be intentional.

Today I challenge myself to ____

____

I proclaim that I ____

RECITE ALL OF THE ABOVE 3 TIMES OUT LOUD

How was your day?

Remember today you just made history. Celebrate you!

A great experience I had today was ____

____

Your future is counting on you to make the most of today. Be optimistic.

A challenge I had today was ____

____

A Win I had today was ____

____

I Dream of ____

SPEND 5 MINUTES MEDITATING ON YOUR DREAMS

Date: ____/ ____/ 20____

Good Morning Sunshine!

Waking up with gratitude cultivates a positive attitude. Think thankful.

I am grateful for ____

____

It makes me happy when ____________________________________

____

The most important thing you can wear is your confidence. Affirm yourself.

I love you ______________________
Your Name

You ____

____

Change is inevitable but growth is by choice. Be intentional.

Today I challenge myself to __________________________________

____

I proclaim that I ____

RECITE ALL OF THE ABOVE 3 TIMES OUT LOUD

How was your day?

Remember today you just made history. Celebrate you!

A great experience I had today was ____________________________

____

Your future is counting on you to make the most of today. Be optimistic.

A challenge I had today was ________________________________

____

A Win I had today was ____________________________________

____

I Dream of ____

SPEND 5 MINUTES MEDITATING ON YOUR DREAMS

Date: ____/ ____/ 20____

Good Morning Sunshine!

Waking up with gratitude cultivates a positive attitude. Think thankful.

I am grateful for ______________________________

____

It makes me happy when ______________________________

____

The most important thing you can wear is your confidence. Affirm yourself.

I love you ______________________________
Your Name

You ______________________________

____

Change is inevitable but growth is by choice. Be intentional.

Today I challenge myself to ______________________________

____

I proclaim that I ______________________________

RECITE ALL OF THE ABOVE 3 TIMES OUT LOUD

How was your day?

Remember today you just made history. Celebrate you!

A great experience I had today was ______________________________

____

Your future is counting on you to make the most of today. Be optimistic.

A challenge I had today was ______________________________

____

A Win I had today was ______________________________

____

I Dream of ______________________________

SPEND 5 MINUTES MEDITATING ON YOUR DREAMS

Date: ____/ ____/ 20____

Good Morning Sunshine!

Waking up with gratitude cultivates a positive attitude. Think thankful.

I am grateful for ______________________________

____

It makes me happy when ______________________________

____

The most important thing you can wear is your confidence. Affirm yourself.

I love you ______________________________
Your Name

You ______________________________

____

Change is inevitable but growth is by choice. Be intentional.

Today I challenge myself to ______________________________

____

I proclaim that I ______________________________

RECITE ALL OF THE ABOVE 3 TIMES OUT LOUD

How was your day?

Remember today you just made history. Celebrate you!

A great experience I had today was ______________________________

____

Your future is counting on you to make the most of today. Be optimistic.

A challenge I had today was ______________________________

____

A Win I had today was ______________________________

____

I Dream of ______________________________

SPEND 5 MINUTES MEDITATING ON YOUR DREAMS

Weekly Recap

• • • • • • • • • •

Don't forget to stop and smell the roses.
-Walter Hagen

Take a moment to reflect on this week's wins and challenges. If you need any personal coaching or guidance I'm only an email away.

valerie@definingiam.com

What was the highlight of your week?

____

____

____

How did you manage your "Focus" for the week?

____

____

____

What were your top 2 Wins this week?

1. ______________________________
2. ______________________________

How did you complete this weeks challenge exercise?

____

____

____

Notes

You Did It!

• • • • • • • • • • •

Congratulations, you have kept your commitment and completed 12 weeks of **The DEFINING I AM Journal**. At this point, I hope you can see some positive changes in your mindset about yourself, your life and your future. You should be in a consistent groove of intentionally championing each day with an attitude of gratitude, self-love, and reflective celebration. This journey isn't easy and won't be perfect, but I am so proud of you for choosing to show up for yourself and making it this far. So go ahead and celebrate this *Win* and treat yourself to the promise you made in your Commitment Statement.

ONE MORE THING...

Before you head off to the mall, remember you've committed to a journey, not a destination. So if you haven't done so already take a few moments to order your next 12-weeks of **The DEFINING I AM Journal**.

www.definingiam.com

Recap With Me

My goal for this journal is to provide you with a tool you can use to impact your life in a positive way. I want you to know that you didn't just buy a journal but also gained a journey companion. I am committed to supporting you and would love to hear how **The DEFINING I AM Journal** has impacted your life. Take a few minutes to recap your overall experience and share with me some of the good, and not so good. I have provided a few questions for you to take into consideration when summarizing your experience. I look forward to hearing from you at valerie@definingiam.com.

-Valerie Richards

ASK YOURSELF

- How has this experience improved your overall mindset?
- How has affirming yourself changed how you feel?
- What personal goals have you accomplished?
- What challenges have you been able to overcome?
- How have you benefited the most from journaling?
- How have you benefited from the weekly challenges?
- What areas did you struggle with?
- What would have improved your overall experience?

Ideas are easy. Execution is everything. It takes a TEAM to WIN.

-John Doerr

Acknowledgments

MY BEST SELF

I want to thank my best self for not giving up on me. For carrying me through the hard times. For pushing me when I wanted to give up. For loving me when I didn't know how to love myself. For teaching me how to believe I can, so I did.

ZIPPORAH MONIQUE & SHOSHANA ROWELL

Zipp & Sho I want to thank you for showing me *it is possible*. Watching you both pursue your dreams inspired me to believe in myself, and go for my own. Thank you for supporting me with making this journal happen. Thank you for cheering me on, holding me accountable and keeping it real. You are Amazing Queens, and I thank God for you both.

MY FOCUS GROUP

Zipporah Monique, Shoshana Rowell, Heather Hatfield, Regina Roberts & Dianne Brown. Thank you ladies for taking the time to support this project and share your feedback. You all are greatly appreciated.

GOD

Thank you for creating me on purpose, with a purpose and for a purpose.

References

5 Benefits of Journaling

Tai Nguyen, (2017). *10 Surprising benefits you'll get from keeping a journal*. Accessed October 2018 through https://www.huffpost.com/entry/benefits-of-journaling_b_6648884

Mindful Staff, (2014). *What is Mindfulness?* Accessed October 2018 through https://www.mindful.org/what-is-mindfulness/

Affirmation Guide

Jack Canfield, (s.d.). *Daily Affirmations for Positive Thinking*. Accessed November 2018 through http://jackcanfield.com/blog/practice-daily-affirmations/

Christopher Lloyd Clarke, (s.d.). *How to Write Affirmations That Really Work*. Accessed November 2018 through https://www.the-guided-meditation-site.com/how-to-write-affirmations.html

The Law of Attraction Library.org, (s.d.). *Examples of Positive Affirmations*. October 2018 through http://thelawofattraction.org/examples-of-positive-affirmations/

Meditation Guide

Ramya Achanta, (April 2, 2018). *Spiritual Meditation – What Is It And What Are Its Benefits?* Accessed November 2018 through https://www.stylecraze.com/articles/simple-steps-to-practice-spiritual-meditation/#gref

Resources

Books

Gillian Anderson and Jennifer Nadel. (2017). WE: A Manifesto for Women Everywhere. (1st. Edition). New York: Atria Books.

Gary John Bishop. (2016). UNFU*K YOURSELF: Get out of your head and into your life. (1st. Edition). New York: Harper Collins Publishers.

Jen Sincero. (2013). You Are a Badass: How to stop doubting your greatness and start living an awesome life. (1st. Edition). Philadelphia, PA: Running Press Book Publishers.

Shannon Kaiser. (2017). The Self-Love Experiment: 15 Principles for Becoming More Kind, Compassionate , and Accepting of Yourself. (1st. Edition). New York: Penguin Random House, LLC.

DEFINING I AM

www.definingiam.com

valerie@definingiam.com

@definingiam

53812769R00104

Made in the USA
Columbia, SC
24 March 2019